John Constable's
ESSEX

Colchester High Street & St Nicholas church, 1830

John Constable's
ESSEX

George Pluckwell

IAN HENRY PUBLICATIONS

ISBN 86025 413 5

The picture on the cover is of the Corn Market, Colchester, 1830. Drawn by W Bartlett and engraved by C Motram.

Printed for
Ian Henry Publications, Ltd.
20 Park Drive, Romford, Essex RM1 4LH
by
WBC Print Ltd, Bristol

INTRODUCTION

Constable Country lies in the valley of the Stour, which flows from four miles northeast of Haverill in Suffolk and follows a tortuous fifty mile course past Sudbury, Wormingford, Boxted, Langham and Dedham, before broadening into an estuary at Manningtree and Mistley and then reaching the North Sea at Harwich.

John Constable, R.A., perhaps the greatest English landscape painter, once said, "I associate my careless boyhood with all that lies on the banks of the Stour. These scenes made me a painter and I am grateful."

Constable was born in East Bergholt, Suffolk, in his father's fine Georgian house, long since demolished, in 1776. Later he attended Dedham Grammar School, painting in his spare time. From school, Constable first went to work in his father's Flatford mill, but his great love of painting drew him to London in about 1797. There he undertook the copying of other artists' work and the study of various techniques. The 17th century Dutch Masters, especially Rubens, Ruysdael and Claude, were an important influence, while other studies included the Suffolk artist Gainsborough. He recognised kindred spirits in the Dutch landscape painters, especially Ruysdael, whose rain-filled clouds and mellow tones made a close parallel with his own work.

1

Rather slow to develop as an original artist, John Constable's remarkable talent was first realised when he exhibited 'Dedham Vale' at the Royal Academy in 1811. Thereafter he devoted himself to his landscapes, taking as his subjects, not only his beloved Stour that was to inspire him for a lifetime, but also Salisbury, Hampstead in north London - where he lived for the latter part of his life, and Brighton.

Constable had numerous Essex connections and travelled to such places as Southend, Southchurch and Hadleigh, as well as in the north-east where he had relations, often with young families - the Robinsons, Parmenters and Constables in Wormingford; Smiths and Masons at Colchester; and more distantly related Constables at Manningtree. There was a constant interchange of visits and the social status of his parents was sufficiently high to allow invitations to dine at the great houses of the neighbourhood.

His sympathetic portrayal of rural scenes is the hallmark of his genius. Those remarkable skies, featuring in some of his works, have often been attributed to his early training as a miller, whose livelihood depends on understanding of the weather.

Constable never made a lot of money nor was he ever wealthy, but, thanks to a few bequests towards the end of his life, he was relieved of his earlier financial anxieties. His wife, Maria, died in 1828, having borne him seven children. For the remainder of his life Constable grieved and sorrowed for her deeply, dying himself in 1837.

The great inspiration of Constable's life and work was the River Stour and in gratitude he wrote, "The sound of water escaping from mill-dams, willows, old rotten planks, slimy posts and brickwork, I love such things. These things made me a painter and I am grateful."

In 1857 several of Constable's paintings reached the Victoria & Albert Museum as a free gift from John

Sheepshanks, who had known the artist. However, the greater bulk of this museum's collection was received in 1888 from Isabel Constable, the artist's last surviving daughter, who had inherited the remains of his studio: her splendid gift of some 400 sketches make the Victoria & Albert the principal single repository of Constable's work. The collection also includes some outstanding finished paintings exhibited at the Royal Academy, the best known being 'Boat Building near Flatford Mill' (1815) and 'Salisbury Cathedral' (1823).

Other examples of his work may be seen at the National Gallery and the Tate in London, while visitors to the Stour area may see some early portraits and drawings, together with some personal relics, at the Minories Art Gallery, High Street, Colchester.

Constable travelled widely through Essex with his sketch books, gaining inspiration for future paintings. Like Fuller writing in 1662, he found "Essex a fair county plentifully affording all things necessary to man's subsistence."

Flatford Mill

SOUTHEND on SEA

Constable seems to have visited Southend on a number of occasions; of course, in his day, South End was simply a small fishing community in the parish of Prittlewell.

The view of Southend from the end of the pier shows, on a clear day, every colour known to the artist's palette. Facing about, one beholds a panorama of unrivalled interest - the 'liquid history' of the Thames, enacted each moment of the day. Small wonder that artists such as Constable found so much to sketch - scenes of the historic, ever-busy estuary.

Constable knew the view from the Kent side, thus looking towards Southend, for in April, 1803, he sailed from London to Deal in the East Indiaman *Coutts,* owned by Captain Torin, a friend of his father. He spent nearly a month on board; when the ship was off Gravesend he walked to Rochester and Chatham and during the voyage he sketched shipping in both Thames and Medway.

There is no mention in C Leslie's biography of Constable of any visit to Leigh on Sea, but in the old High Street there was a shop over which, it is confidently claimed locally, he lodged for some days - a drawing of this house by 'Quip' appeared some years ago in the *Southend Standard.* The claim seems reasonable for, from just such a position at the back of these premises, John

4

Constable must have made some of his sketches of craft on the Thames. From the most western point of Marine Parade, Leigh, there is also a good view of the ruins of Hadleigh Castle, once the great stronghold of Hubert de Burgh, to whom the property was granted by Henry III. In a letter to his friend, Dunthorne, telling of his river trip (May, 1803) there is no mention of these ruins, but he must have seen them. A letter to his ladylove and future wife, Maria Bicknell, in 1814, merely states that he had been to Hadleigh, where he adds "there is a ruin of a castle, which from its situation is vastly fine. It commands a view of the Kent hills, the Nore, and the North Foreland, looking many miles to sea." It was not until April, 1829, that he wrote to Leslie saying that he had forwarded his picture 'Hadleigh Castle', asking if he should exhibit it. This he did the same year and it was eventually engraved by David Lucas, and others since. The picture in question – he executed several other studies of the same subject was exhibited at the Grosvenor Gallery, London, in 1888.

Hubert de Burgh (d. 1243) was Chief Judiciar of England and figures in Shakespeare's *King John,* Act IV, on the strength of a story derived from Ralph de Coggeshall. De Burgh was Judiciar in June, 1215, the month Magna Carta was signed at Runnymede and there is evidence that de Burgh played an influential part in obtaining it. His name occurs on the list of the barons who upheld the 25 Conservators of the Charter. In 1216 he vigorously defended Dover Castle, in his other role as Earl of Kent, against the French and was obliged to make a truce with Louis. Under Henry III he commanded the first English fleet to win a naval battle by destroying the French fleet off North Foreland.

In 1219, on the death of the Regent, de Burgh assumed much power and began building Hadleigh Castle, but within a year, and with walls only just rising, he was banished from Royal Favour. King Henry III took charge of the Castle, had it completed, and appointed a

Governor - who throughout seven reigns had to entertain royal hunting parties or expeditions in the dense woods surrounding Hadleigh.

In the 14th century Edward III virtually rebuilt the Castle as a deterrent against raiding French who sailed up the Thames.

The Castle and lands were settled as a dower on many English queens, including three wives of Henry VIII, one being Anne of Cleves. By then it had grown old and decrepit, so Lord Rich stepped in and purchased it for £700 from Edward VI in 1551. He used it only as a quarry from which stone could be reclaimed for other building work. Lord Rich's workmen did a thorough job and a landslide carried away the south wall and all that side of Hadleigh Castle - not overlooking a range of domestic buildings.

On his second trip to Southend in 1814, Constable accompanied the Rev Walter Wren Driffield, a 70-year-old man from Constable's neighbourhood. Immediately after graduating from Cambridge in 1767 he had been presented with the living of Erwarton with Woolverstone, in Suffolk and, seven years later by the Archbishop of Canterbury, to that of Southchurch in Essex. But, like other clergymen of his time who seemed to make a practice of exchanging parishes, he preferred to live elsewhere. At the time of Constable's birth he was living at East Bergholt and thus it happened that he was summoned hastily one night to baptize John, who was not expected to live. When he went to Southend with Constable he was residing at Feering, west of Colchester.

A full account of Constable's visit is given in a letter John wrote to Maria Bicknell. From this we learn that he had promised to make Mr Driffield a drawing of his Feering house. As the rector had occasion to visit his parish of Southchurch it was suggested that Constable go too, thereby giving him an opportunity of seeing a part of Essex, bordering on the Thames estuary, he had never seen before. Constable took with him a small sketch book in which to make memoranda of the places he visited and, although his host was so active that he found little time for sketching, he managed to fill it with drawings. On the evening of 23rd June he was able to take advantage of Mr Driffield's absence on parochial matters to wander about, alone, on the beach near Southend.

Later Constable writing from East Bergholt to Miss Bicknell in July, 1814, said, "I have been absent from this place more than a fortnight, on a visit to the Rev Driffield, at Feering, near Kelvedon. He is a very old friend of my father's and once christened me in great haste about eleven o'clock. During my visit I accompanied him to South Church by which I saw much more of the county of Essex than I had ever seen before, and the most beautiful part of it, as I was at Maldon, Rochford, South End, Hadleigh, Danbury, etc. I have filled as usual a little book of hasty memoranda of the places which I saw.

"There are times when I was so delighted with the scenery as to forget that my mind had been so long a stranger to happiness."

Among Constable's water-colour sketches now in private hands is one entitled 'Feering Church'. Perhaps this is the picture executed for Rev Driffield.

A list of the Rectors of Southchurch shows that Walter Wren Driffield held the living from 1774 to 1828. Southchurch was a pleasant village of a few hundred population, on sloping ground, with a fine south view over the Thames. It was one and a half miles east of Southend. The church, dedicated to the Holy Trinity, was a small stone building that was restored in 1856. The church plate dates from 1682 and the registers from 1695.

There is an Eagle Pond here, which is public property and is, in the summer, much frequented by anglers. At least, that was the picture in 1887 in Durrants handy *Essex Guide*.

7

In 1816 Constable paid a visit to Mr Driffield, again at Feering. The thoughtful parson kindly offered to help him over his marriage problems, and they may have made a second excursion to Southchurch. A drawing of Feering in the Fitzwilliam Museum is dated 26th July, 1816, and one of Hadleigh Castle seems to belong to that same year.

Maria Bicknell's father, Charles, opposed the marriage of his daughter to John Constable; so did her grandfather, the Rector of East Bergholt, the Rev Dr Rhuddle. This situation appears very strange to us today, as Miss Bicknell was 29 years old and Constable was in his 40th year. It seems to have been the classic story of a well-off young lady and a struggling artist. Dr Rhuddle considered it an unthinkably disadvantageous match.

John Constable and Maria Bicknell were married in London on 2nd October, 1816. Although Constable had written a respectful letter to Dr Rhuddle telling him of his intentions, the letter remained unanswered. The family clearly could not reconcile themselves to Maria marrying beneath her. They felt he was not earning enough to support or keep a wife – far less a family. John and Maria left for Southampton in accordance with a plan they had previously discussed, perhaps staying with Constable's favourite relations, the Gubbins family. They later went on to spend six weeks at Osmington Vicarage, near Weymouth, with their young friends, the Rev John Fisher and his young wife of only a few months.

Southend first came into notice through some royal visitors in 1804. For, one year after Constable's first visit, Queen Caroline came, with her daughter, Princess Charlotte, after which Southend became a fashionable watering place. Queen Caroline of Brunswick had been married to George IV in 1795, when he was still Prince of Wales. They only lived together for a short time and had one daughter. When the Prince Regent finally ascended the throne in 1820 the Queen took steps to assert her position and the King retaliated by having a Bill introduced to dissolve the marriage. She was locked out of Westminster Abbey on the Coronation Day and died soon afterwards, some say of a broken heart.

The population of Southend has increased in a remarkable fashion. In 1871 it was only 2,808; by 1901 it had reached 28,857; and in the 1940s it soared to 136,000. The bathing is good, although the sea recedes nearly a mile.

The old wooden pier was replaced in 1890 by one of iron and, by 1898, it was one and a half miles in length. Until a devastating fire a few years ago it was claimed to be the longest pier in the world. In the Edwardian period the pier was an ideal promenading place. An electric tramway ran the entire length of the pier, being intended originally to carry passengers and their luggage to the steamships at the pier head; during the summer months these boats plied between Southend and London, Sheerness, Rochester and Gravesend. Until the 1950s the Golden Eagle steamships sailed between Tower Bridge, London and Margate on the Kent coast, docking mid-way at Southend. To be on board was to imagine you were going on a real ocean voyage!

Southend Pier tramway later became an electric railway, carrying thousands of holidaymakers in the summer season. The old stock was sold to Vokes Railway in Brighton, but the pier railway has now been restored and refurbished.

The illuminations in the autumn were something to behold and competed with Blackpool in the north. Thousands of electric light bulbs were used to create this wonderland. The whole promenade was hung with miles of fairy lights, strung like a crystal necklace or threaded stars. Pictures and patterns of all varieties mingled together on the sea front. There were special coach trips organised from London to see the 'Southend Lights'.

In John Constable's day transport was either the

stagecoach, sometimes a long bumpy journey in a gig, on horseback or, maybe, by boat. In the Victoria era the pioneer railway companies ran steam trains from Liverpool Street and Fenchurch Street Stations in London. In the 1960s advertisements read, "British Rail serves, by fast and frequent electric service to Southend": also "For local passengers the fare between the station and the airport of one shilling [5p]."

In 1933 Southend Corporation purchased the land from which in the 1914-18 War squadrons of the Royal Flying Corps flew against the German Zeppelins and Gothas. The Air Ministry later established a unit of the R.A.F. here, a Volunteer Reserve Group. In 1940 it reverted to being a military airfield from where Churchill's 'illustrious few' battled with the Luftwaffe. In 1947 the Corporation opened the civil airport and licensed traffic.

Southend was incorporated in 1892 and, until the reorganisation of local government in 1974, was a 'county borough' with a Mayor, aldermen and councillors. It became an ecclesiastical parish in 1842 after the Church of St John the Baptist was built in 1840, it has been enlarged since then in 1869, 1873 and 1912.

George Sherrin, the much neglected Victorian architect, built the Kursaal pleasure grounds and park between 1898 and 1902. He also designed houses for Southend's Beresford Road. His other Essex achievements were the College Hospital at Halstead (1884) and Alexandra Hotel, Dovercourt - now flats (1903).

Sherrin was born in London in 1843 and at the age of 16 was articled to a firm of architects near King's Cross. He moved to Chelmsford and qualified in the 1860s in the office of Frederic Chancellor, a prominent architect. Sherrin was also an artist and his drawings were exhibited at the Royal Academy on a few occasions. Later he was appointed Chief Architect of the Kursaal site of 26 acres containing a ballroom (like a Wren church) for 1,400 people; 53 houses; and 90 shops.

Sadly, some of this amusement and pleasure park has now been demolished for a housing estate.

Personal memories of Southend stretch back over 40 years. I recall the 1950s and Cockneys on a day trip from London doing a 'Knees up, Mother Brown,' outside the numerous public houses; and the old jellied eel stalls and pie and mash shops. Holidaymakers visiting the life-size model of Drake's *Golden Hind* - perhaps dreaming of voyages to other lands. The silver domed towers of the Kursaal - glittering in the sunlight like far Indian pavilions - holding the giant scenic railway, the water-chute and the wall of death, where a motor-cyclist raced round a wooden wall at a terrific speed in daredevil style.

Old Leigh is closer to London, but Londoners tend to visit bigger, brasher Southend. Leigh is renowned for its famous cockles. It has escaped the worst of the ravages of development and still retains much of its charm from the days when it was an important seafaring community.

The 500 year old St Clement's Church is dedicated to the saint who was martyred by being thrown into the sea bound to an anchor. Sailors from Leigh were on Drake's and Horrey's ships when they set out to find new lands for Queen Elizabeth - and to fight the Spaniards.

The port traded with France and the Netherlands in the 16th century, a fleet of forty ships carrying goods to and from Leigh. But gradually the harbour silted up and Leigh became a safe haven for small fishing boats, who combined a little smuggling with the main trade of fishing. When the Peter Boat Inn caught fire in last century a large underground room with its own waterside entrance, still containing remains of contraband, was discovered. In old Leigh there is a fine selection of historical inns.

Southend has the Beecroft Art Gallery in Station Road, displaying eight galleries of British and European paintings; it is free to the public. Prittlewell Museum in Priory Park is in the Refectory of old Prittlewell Priory.

In this modern age Southend has varied light industry and the population has exploded to over 170,000 and is still rising.

Constable can have the last words: "It will be difficult to name a class of landscape in which the sky is not the key note, the standard scale, and the chief organ of sentiment."

After a stroll on the beach at Southend, Constable also wrote, "I was always delighted with the melancholy grandeur of a sea shore."

Southend-o

Hotel Metropole and Queen Victoria's Statue.

Southend

Southend Pier Head. c.1890

THE RIVER STOUR

Certain navigation works in the freshwater parts of the Stour were authorised in patents of the early 17th century, but the modern history of the improvements dates from 1705. In that year an Act of Parliament empowered the Corporation of Sudbury, Suffolk, to carry out navigation works. Golding Constable, John's father, was made one of the members of the Stour Navigation Commission when the Act was revised in 1781.

Golding's business was then centred round Flatford Mill (Suffolk) and Dedham (Essex) on the Stour. Access had been difficult for larger boats as the river had become silted up and shallow. Now it was made navigable for barge traffic from Sudbury to Manningtree and Mistley. This meant that, instead of carting flour from the Stourside mills inland by bad roads to Mistley Docks and then by ship from the London trade, he could now send the milled flour by barge downstream to Mistley and thence to the capital.

The navigation works were of a crude pattern; the thirteen locks between Sudbury and Brantham and the thirteen additional flash locks were entirely of timber construction. Sudbury was the head of these developments and had a basin, wharves and warehouses. The mills on the Stour, like Wormingford, had cuts and wharves where lighters could load and unload. This benefited the mills on the Essex side of the river and places like Boxted, Langham and Dedham grew prosperous.

The wooden barges or lighters that Constable loved to paint were constructed in a basin at Flatford. They were towed by pairs of horses over a distance of nearly 24 miles between Sudbury and Brantham Tidal Lock, where they were floated on the tide for a further 3 miles to Mistley Quay. They measured about 47 feet long by 10 feet, 9 inches, across the beam, drawing about 2 feet, 9 inches, when loaded with 13 tons.

Horses pulled the paired barges assisted by the bargees with long handled poles known as quants. Sometimes a square sail was hoisted if the wind was in the right direction. They were built and manned by people of the East Anglian breed, some of whom spent the whole of their working lives transporting goods on the River Stour. Flour, bricks, chalk, lime and agricultural products were carried to Mistley Docks and thus the production of a whole area of inland Suffolk and Essex had a cheap route to London.

The Stour lighters and horses were often featured in Constable's paintings: they, like the smaller boats and timber locks, were a favourite subject. Constable's 'White Horse', painted in 1819, showed a common enough picture in these parts, where the tow-path crossed from one bank to the other, so that the barge horses had to be ferried across the cut. His 'Leaping Horse' (1824) is a scene near Dedham, with a boy taking a barge-horse over one of the barriers erected on the tow-path to prevent cattle from straying. This stretch of river was known as 'the canal', being separated from the main branch of the Stour.

The navigation was run successfully and became very prosperous, carrying 100,000 tons annually in its heyday. By 1848 the average income over five years was £52,918, against expenditure of £750. But the threat of railway competition was becoming apparent and the shares of the undertaking were offered to the railway company building the Stour Valley line at £1,000 each. This was refused.

By 1924 navigation only continued up the river to Dedham. In 1927 the revised Bill of South Essex Waterworks Company was served and the Navigation Company succeeded in reaching a more favourable settlement than was available under the first draft Bill. In consideration of the Navigation Company withdrawing all opposition to the Bill, the Waterworks Company would rebuild, to modern standards, the four lower locks of Brantham, Flatford, Dedham and Stratford St Mary. They were to maintain them and allow sufficient water through for river traffic. This agreement was duly signed and sealed; the plans and specifications of the new locks approved; and work commenced.

Meanwhile navigation had ceased, for the last working barge left Dedham in 1928 and the Navigation Company was never to reap the benefits of the rebuilt locks. In 1935 the company's solicitor advised that, in view of the financial position, it should be dissolved. Whether the company could do this in respect of their responsibilities as Trustees is unclear. In November, 1935, a most unusual General Meeting was held, when it was resolved that the said company should be wound up and struck off the Register of Companies. The following April the Secretary reported that, in accordance with a note inserted in the *London Gazette* dated 16th March, the Company ceased to exist.

A certain amount of maintenance was still carried out by on the new river locks by the waterworks, but this too eventually came to a halt.

In 1974 the Anglian Water Authority took over the functions previously administered by the Essex River Authority on the River Stour. They have extra responsibilities, including a requirement to take into account recreation, the conservation of amenities and wildlife.

16

A private Act of Parliament has enabled them to become the navigation authority.

There are no known records of navigation on the Stour by commercial boats, other than the cargo barges, but many small privately-owned boats have used the river, like those shown in nearly every Constable painting of the Stour.

Today the Inland Waterways Association does much to preserve the nation's rivers and canals, including the Stour. The River Stour Trust exists to safeguard and promote the recreational use of the river for the benefit and enjoyment of the community at large. In 1975 the Trust started repairing Flatford Lock, after receiving official permission to do so and, subsequently, organised voluntary weekend working parties to remove tons of silt from the chamber, make the lock gates watertight and renovate the operating mechanism, besides a general 'tidy-up' of the area. The re-opened lock enables craft to pass readily from the North Sea up-river to Dedham, a distance of three miles.

In 1985 the Trust unearthed a Stour barge at Flatford, similar to that in Constable's famous barge painting, 'Boat Building near Flatford Mill, 1814' (Victoria & Albert Museum). Identification of the barge will be difficult: it is known that many barges were deliberately scuttled in 1914, just before the war, as an anti-invasion tactic. The National Trust is helping to preserve this barge as a living part of the history of the Stour Navigation and, of course, its associations with Constable.

There was more good news in 1985: a new 80 foot wooden footbridge was lifted into position across the Stour between Dedham and Flatford. This is on the site of Constable's favourite bridge by which he used to go to school from East Bergholt to Dedham and which collapsed in 1930. The new bridge cost £14,000, raised by grants and donations.

Over two hundred years ago the great historian and topographer, John Norden, visited this north-east corner of Essex and observed it was 'most fatte, fruteful and full of profitable things, exceeding (as far as I can finde) anie other shire for general commodities and plenty... This shire seemeth to me to deserve the title of the Englishe Goshen, the fattest of the Lands, comparable to Palestina that flowed with milke and hunnye.'

The language might sound a little extravagant to modern ears, but Stourside has all these things. A variety of wildlife, both birds and mammals, can be observed; in the reedbed localities, particularly the damp wooded areas, there are innumerable species of insects; amphibian life is also found, both common frogs and toads and crested newts and lizards. Sometimes on the grassy banks may be seen an adder or a grass-snake. Ditches and tiny tributaries from the farmlands provide ideal nesting places for small birds and animals. They say Constable lay so still in a field near Dedham, taking in nature's scenery for his pictures, that a field-mouse crept into his pocket.

Ducks are plentiful and the mallards are always there, joined by the tufted and, often, the domestic Aylesbury; their activities and splashings delighting the visitor. Such fish as bream, perch and the marauding pike are to be found; the angling clubs responsible for fishing rights keep a keen eye on the quality and quantity of the stock and contribute to the river's conservation.

In the summer the Stour attracts thousands of visiting warblers to mix with the housemartins and swallows, who enjoy a dip and drink, as they wing low along the course of the glittering river.

The fine mute swan is a regular visitor to picnic areas like Henny Weir and Ballingdon Bridge, while numbers exceeding 150 have been seen at Manningtree. Another popular inhabitant is the heron, common over the entire length of the river, while upstream in the ivy-covered banks, where willowherb and nettles abound, small ground mammals are found - our lesser or pygmy shrew, bank voles and the much rarer water shrew.

Roe deer ofter visit the upper reaches in the early morning for water and, evocative of *Wind in the Willows,* badgers are sometimes seen near the river, perhaps looking for friend 'Ratty'. An otter may sometimes be seen along the middle or lower reaches, although sadly this creature is now very rare in East Anglia.

So Stourside is a naturalists' retreat that can be enjoyed and appreciated by all seeking a quiet haven in this modern world.

Constable wrote: "Light - dews - breezes - bloom - and freshness, not one of which has yet been perfected on the canvas of any painter in the world."

RIVER AND OLD COTTAGE, FLATFORD.   G.9718

Flatford

WORMINGFORD

Wormingford is a village six miles from Colchester, covering 331 acres. The population in Victorian times was 477 - in Constable's day it was even less.

Constable's Uncle Abram (Golding's younger brother) dwelt at Gernons Farm and his first wife was Mary Kingsbury of Wormingford. Abram had acquired the tenancy of Gernons Farm in 1741 and John spent long holidays at Gernons painting.

In a letter dated 22nd February, 1813, Constable's mother, Ann, writing from his parents' splendid Georgian house at East Bergholt mentions his cousin, Sarah (later Mrs Coker): "Sarah Constable is now with us. She told me the Nayland Altar piece looks nicely when the sun shines on it [John's sacred study of Christ's blessing of the Bread and Wine at Nayland, Suffolk] I want it to look nicely always in truth I want you and all your performances to be nothing short of perfection.

"Golding has a bad cold, very hoarse, caught it at Wormingford, where himself, Abram, Nancy and Mary were last Wednesday." Ann refers here to some of Golding's two brothers and three sisters, of whom he was the fourth child.

John's sister, Mary, in a letter from Flatford Mill to him at Hampstead in 1835 wrote of Sarah - "Sarah (Mrs

Coker) has lost her poor distracted and distracting husband and I fear her own health is failing seriously, with water on the chest. You know - poor woman - she inherits 'dropsy' and she has had a heavy share of war and afflictions to struggle with for several years past. She has one living child, a son [Sidey, who married Ann Garrod]."

Uncle Abram was married twice. His second wife was Mary Sidey of nearby Bures; they had one son named John Sidey Constable, who would have been Sarah's step-brother.

John Sidey (he was always called that by the family) worked as a mariner, apparently engaged in transporting flour from Mistley to the London Docks. He was employed on the sailing ship the *Telegraph*. Both the yard at Mistley and the ship were owned by Golding Constable, so it appears that he was working in the Constable milling and transport business.

In Domesday times Wormingford was called Wither-mundford or Wethermundeford, the name being derived from an ancient proprietor of the manor and a local ford across the Stour. It was also spelt Wildemondfont, Wyre-mundeford and Mormiton.

In Edward the Confessor's time the manor was held by the Earl Godwin, father of Harold II, who reigned for nine months before the Conquest. By the time of the Norman survey the manor was held by Robert Gernon and looked after by Ilger, his Thane. The manors and lands of Wormingford cover 1,700 acres.

Wormingford Hall Manor, a mile west of the church, and the Barony of Stansted Mountfitchet were held by Richard de Plaiz until he died without issue. Then his rich estate was divided between three sisters, of whom Philippa, the youngest, married Hugh de Plaiz (perhaps a cousin) and brought him this estate. His descendants successively were Richard, Ralph, Giles and John, whose only daughter, Margaret, through marriage to Sir John Howard, took the Wormingford Lordships of the Manor into the Howard family. They had two children, John – who died before his father – and Elizabeth, who became sole heiress. She married John de Vere, heir of Richard, Earl of Oxford.

The Essex historian, Morant, wrote, "The de Veres, Earls of Oxford, were one of the most ancient and illustrious families in England, if not the world." They owned estates in ten counties and were among the rose of English chivalry during the Hundred Years War. Alberic de Vere, a Norman knight thought to have been the Lord of Ver (south of Coutance in the La Manche region of Normandy), had come over with William the Conqueror and was given fourteen Lordships in Essex, as well as land in Suffolk, Huntingdon and Cambridge. London, even today, bears traces of the famous family in names like Earl's Court (where the de Veres had their court-house) and De Vere Gardens in Kensington, where he held the Lordship of the Manor. He founded Colne Priory at Earl's Colne in 1105. Many of the Earls of Oxford were buried within the Priory grounds or walls. Alberic (or Aubrey) married Beatrice, half sister of King William, and they had five sons. After her death he became a monk at the Priory.

Aubrey II, their eldest son, built the magnificent Castle Hedingham, which remained in the family for 550 years and was visited by Elizabeth I. The architect is said to be William de Corbeuil, Archbishop of Canterbury, who built the walls twelve feet thick in places and faced them with Ashlar stone brought from the quarries of Barnack in Northamptonshire. Few Norman castles were faced with stone like Hedingham, normally only doorways and windows could be afforded, as there were few nobles as wealthy or powerful as the de Veres, who could stand the tremendous cost. The keep is in a splendid state of preservation and is a hundred feet high. It is approached by a Tudor bridge spanning the now dry moat. In the Banqueting Hall, once strewn with rushes and with its walls ablaze with fine decorated hangings, there is a gallery where once minstrels and troubadours played. This Great Hall can also boast a Norman ceiling arch, the largest in Europe.

Aubrey married Alice Fitz Richard of Clare, daughter of the Earl of Hertford. Aubrey was called 'The King's Chamberlain' in 1112 and was created Lord Great Chamberlain of England in 1133. He attended King Stephen's coronations at Westminster and Winchester in 1136. His daughter, Rohesia, wed Geoffrey de Mandeville, the first Earl of Essex, and it is believed that this association (Essex was unpopular in London) caused Aubrey's untimely death in a London riot in 1141.

His son, Aubrey III, was a Crusader and was created Earl of Oxford by Queen Matilda (or Maud). She offered him the choice of title - Cambridge ("provided the King of Scots had it not"), Oxford, Wiltshire or of other counties. He picked Oxford, a title that endured for twenty generations. Queen Matilda came to end her royal days at Hedingham and died there in 1151.

The 2nd Earl of Oxford, another Aubrey, fought with Richard Coeur de Lion in Normandy and later commanded King John's forces in Ireland. He was a Privy Councillor and was made Steward of the Forests of Essex. He died childless and his brother, Robert, inherited.

Robert de Vere, 3rd Earl, was also a Crusader. In the fifteenth year of John's reign Robert, with 25 other barons, took up arms against the King 'in defence of the liberties of England' and forced him to sign the Magna Carta in 1215. For this he was excommunicated and the barons offered the Crown of England to Louis, son of the King of France (the Dauphin). King John attacked and a battle followed with the French surrendering. He then laid seige to Hedingham Castle, which fell to him at Lent in 1216, after lengthy and fierce resistance. After John's death peace was made between the new King, Henry II, and the warring barons and Oxford was back in favour. All his lands were restored to him, including Hedingham.

Returning to the Wormingford connection, Elizabeth Howard married John de Vere, 12th Earl of Oxford, who succeeded in 1417 when he was only nine years old. He was a prominent Lancastrian and loyal to King Henry VI. Unfortunately, with the accession of Edward IV and the ascendancy of the Yorkists, he and his eldest son were arrested at Castle Hedingham and imprisoned in the Tower of London. These were terrible times for the de Veres, for in 1461 both were beheaded on Tower Hill, Aubrey, the son, going to the block in full view of his father.

The 12th Earl's second son, John, the 13th Earl, was probably the richest of all the de Veres. He was only 19 when his father and brother were executed. Like his father he supported the Lancastrian cause and received most of his honours for leadership and courage in the Wars of the Roses, playing a prominent part in placing Henry VII on the throne.

On one occasion he entertained the King to a sumptuous banquet at Hedingham Castle. On leaving, the King asked the Earl if those he saw present were his servants. He was told they were the Earl's retainers. Henry had passed a law prohibiting the maintenance of such persons and was startled at the impudence of the reply. The King could not enduring having his laws thus broken and a fine of 15,000 marks (£10,000) was imposed!

The 13th Earl died in 1512 and was laid to rest in the same tomb as his first wife, Margaret, sister of the Earl of Warwick, in Colne Priory.

The lifestyle of the de Veres would fill a volume. They adopted the five pointed star as their emblem and this star or 'mullet', as it is called, illuminated on their standard brought them great victory in the First Crusade against the Saracens in 1098. This emblem is seen on many churches and other buildings in Essex and Suffolk connected with the family, for example in Earl's Colne church. Their arms, quarterly gules and or, in the first quarter a mullet argent, are amongst the simplest and best-known in heraldry.

Later the Manor came to the Poynings, Bauds and various other tenants. The Waldegraves were, for a long time, Lords of this estate and it eventually passed to Jack Currants. Wormingford Hall formerly had a park, farm and lodge.

Church House was another Wormingford Manor, usually referred to as the 'Manor House of Church Hall'. It was granted to the nuns of Wilkes in the reign of Plantagenet Henry II (1154-80) by Walter Windlesores and Christiana, his mother. Henry VIII granted the Manor and nunnery to his favourite, Cardinal Wolsey and, upon suppression of the monasteries, it progressed into the hands of Thomas Monok and, later, the Waldegraves.

Wolsey was the son of an Ipswich butcher and lived from 1473 until 1530. Showing great ability he was sent to Oxford University and, on entering the Church, rose to a position of eminence. He was entrusted with several diplomatic missions and was especially favoured by Henry VIII. Under this monarch he secured rapid preferment, being in turn Bishop of Lincoln and Archbishop of York. He was Henry's Chancellor and founded a great College at Ipswich, which was demolished after his fall from grace. For a number of years he was supreme and, by his diplomacy, did much to strengthen the kingly power. But when Wolsey was unable, though willing enough, to obtain the papal sanction of Clement VII for Henry's divorce from his first wife, Catherine of Aragon, he fell into disfavour and his decline was rapid indeed. From being a great personage with a princely entourage, he was humbled, persecuted, and harried and died at Leicester Abbey a broken, dejected man, soon after being summoned to London and the Tower for treason.

Gernons was a smaller Wormingford manor, taking its name from an ancient owner of the estate. It was a mansion and was moated round at the lower end of the park, near the Stour. William Gernon, the early owner, died in 1229 and one of his descendants, Sir John Gernon, left it to his two daughters in 1383 as co-heiresses. One, named Joan, married Sir John Peyton; so the Manor Lordship carried on through the female line and their husbands, like so many other Essex manors. There were families like the Helions, Fyndernes, and the Wentworths, all of whom must have done their share in shaping Essex history.

The church of St Andrew is chiefly of 13th century style, with a south aisle and a square tower housing four bells. It was thoroughly restored in 1869/70.

The area today is still agricultural, having several farms and an ancient inn called The Crown. The Queen's Head opened in the fourth year of Victoria's reign.

During World War II there was a military airfield at Wormingford; some of the corrugated iron hangers, once sheltering Spitfires, are now used for more peaceful purposes as barns and stables.

There is a reasonable bus service running through Wormingford from Colchester to Sudbury by Eastern National and Chambers of Bures - a small private bus company.

The Stour is clearly seen and is conspicuous at Wormingford Mere, a large sheet of water surrounded by trees. The river at Wormingford Mill is lovely; here are the Mill House, the tumbling sluices and the mill pool surrounded by great willow trees. Wormingford Mill once belonged to Wormingford Manor and stood beside the ford. It was a high structure of Essex boards, painted white and with a roof of red tiles. In 1879 it was bought by C Hitchcock and was burnt down in 1929. After the destruction of the mill the great wheel gradually slid into the river and there it lay submerged until the 1939-45 War, when it was salvaged as scrap-iron. A sad end to a fine and useful mill. Immediately below the sparkling pool is Wormingford Bridge. The navigation formerly bypassed Wormingford Mill by an artificial cut about a third of a mile long in which were Wormingford and Swan Locks. The cut is now dry and overgrown, but the remains of the locks Constable probably saw are still in evidence. Swan Lock shows particularly clearly the construction of the old wooden locks, with their timbered sides, that he took so much delight in painting.

Constable said: "My limited and abstracted art is to be found under every hedge and in every lane, and therefore nobody thinks it worth picking up."

Wormingford is full of historical houses, mostly well preserved and restored. A house called Bottengoms is constructed of wattle and daub, with a timber frame: it is much older than its 17th century chimney. Once a farmstead it lay derelict for a few years until bought and restored to become a private residence. It was lived in for a number of years by the Essex artist, John Nash, R.A., who painted from the garden, many of his paintings carrying the variations of green which so fascinated him in the surrounding grass and trees. He died in 1977 and the new owner was Ronald Blythe, the author of many books, including the famous *Akenfield*.

I must mention the strange story of the Wormingford Dragon. Legend says that the Crusader king, Richard I, was given the gift of a crocodile by Saladin. This was housed in the Tower of London, amongst the King's Beasts, but escaped into the marshy lands of Essex. The only written record is the tale of a monk, John de Trokelowe, amongst the 1401 St Alban papers at Cambridge. It states –

> Close to the town of Bures there has lately appeared a dragon vast in body with a crested head, teeth like a saw and tail extending to an enormous length. Having slaughtered the shepherd it devoured very many sheep. Then came an order to shoot at him with arrows, to workmen on whose domain he had concealed himself being Sir Richard de Waldegrave, Knight, of Wormingford. But the dragon, although struck by the archers, remained unhurt, for the arrows

bounced off his back as if it had been iron or hard rock. All the country people assemebled and there was an order to destroy him. But when the dragon saw he was again to be assaulted he fled away into a marsh or mere and was seen no more."

It was significant that the name of Withermundeforde was changed in the Middle Ages to Wormingford, for Worm was the name for a dragon or beast. In the church one can view the Dragon Window, which was given by Maria M Boggis-Rolfe in gratitude to God for the men and women who returned from the Second World War. It is modern and the delicate colouring and overall lightness reflect the work of present-day craftsmen.

Lighters at Wormingford, c.1900

BOXTED

Boxted is a village on the south of the Stour, only four miles from Colchester. All over Essex there is a Constable connection and nowhere stronger than here. For in tracing the artist's ancestry, one need go no further back than William Constable, a yeoman, of Boxted, who died in 1667, leaving a son named John, yeoman of Little Bromley, near Mistley.

This John was, in turn, father of the artist's great-grandfather, Hugh, who was born in the year of his grandfather, William's, death. Hugh would, no doubt, have been greatly surprised to be told that his own descendants would one day take him for the son of a Yorkshire baronet. He had, in fact, migrated from the place where he was born and, after some wanderings, settled down to farm land in or near Mount Bures. On his death, in 1715, he left four sons, two of whom remained on the land, while the other two left to go into business with remarkable success.

Hugh's third son was the second John Constable, born in 1705. He was a farmer and landowner at Bures St Mary on the Suffolk side. He was also Lord of the Manor of Kemsings in right of his wife, Judith Garrad of Bures, who was heiress through her mother of the Goldings of Cavendish, a very old family in those parts. John

29

Constable of Bures died in 1777 leaving eight children surviving of a family of ten. The sixth child, born on 18th February, 1739 and named after his grandmother's family, was Golding, father of the famous John.

However, to return to the delightful village of Boxted; there is a fine view across the Stour, with the tower of Stoke-by-Nayland church, Suffolk, visible in the distance. The church of St Peter, Boxted, described in the 1909 edition of Cox's *Essex Guide* as 'a poor and much over-restored fabric' contains a monument to Elizabeth, wife of Nathaniel Bacon, 1628, and another of marble with a long inscription in Latin verse to Sir Richard Blackmore, 1729, physician in ordinary to William III and Queen Anne. Blackmore, known chiefly by Johnson's *Life* of him, was the 'everlasting Blackmore' of the *Dunciad*, so dubbed for his prolific writings. He published several epics, for example *Prince Arthur* and *The Creation.* In the *Tatler*, Steele made fun of Blackmore, who studied at Oxford and Padua and was a Fellow of the College of Physicians, but retired to Boxted in 1722. The Norman church tower holds the record for having more 'puddingstone' in its construction than any other tower in East Anglia.

Boxted figures in what was called the 'Dedham Classis', which body met here in March 1582/3. Their Minute Book (1582-9) was published by the Royal Historical Society in 1905 from the record in the possession of J F Gurney of Keswick Hall, Norfolk. The nature of this classis may be shown by the Minute Book being published to illustrate the Presbyterian movement in the reign of Elizabeth I.

No-one seems to know for certain the origin of the name 'Boxted'. There are many suggestions - like Bocsted, Bocchesteda and Buchestede, besides others like Borstad and Borstened. Even Wright's *History of Essex* fails to clarify how this village came by its name.   It is nine miles in circumference and, at the time of Edward the Confessor, was held by one Aluric, who would have been a Saxon. At the Domesday survey the two large manors of Boxted were held by two most powerful Normans - Eustace, Earl of Boulogne, and Eudo Dapifer, William the Conqueror's High Steward.

The first Manor, Boxted Hall, is half a mile west of the church. In the reign of Henry I and Stephen, the Manor was held by Everard de Boxted for the Earl of Boulogne. Robert de Naunton held it in fee-tail of King Henry VI in 1445 and by 1531 it was in the hands of Sir John Strangway, cousin and co-heir of Lord Scrope, of whom it was purchased by G W Maleverer. It was conveyed without the King's licence, for which he was obliged to procure a pardon. It passed on to Lord Thomas Cromwell in 1539 and, on his fall, to the Pooleys.

Cromwell was originally a protègè of Wolsey and rose to high office under Henry VIII. He began the suppression of the monasteries, but was executed for high treason after the failure of the Anne of Cleves marriage, which had been arranged as part of the policy of alliance with the Protestant princes of Germany. Anne agreed to a divorce from the King and lived to a ripe old age in retirement at London and Bradwell-on-Sea in Essex amongst other places.

The Lordship of the Manor of Boxted Hall passed through many hands until it was bought in the 17th century by Paul, Viscount Bayning, who gave it to his daughter, Anne, on her marriage to Aubrey de Vere, 20th Earl of Oxford. This Aubrey de Vere had been born in London in 1627 and by 1660 he was appointed Lord Lieutenant of Essex and also made Colonel of the Royal Regiment of Horse (from then known as Oxford's Horse or Oxford's Blues), now the Horse Guards. He bore the Sword of State at the Coronation of James II and the King, needing an obedient Parliament, tried to use the Lords Lieutenant of the counties to ensure the return of picked men. When the King asked Oxford his intentions, Aubrey replied, "Sire, I will stand by your Majesty against all enemies to the last drop of my blood, but this is a matter of conscience and I cannot comply."

James was displeased and Oxford's regiment was taken from him and Lord Petre replaced him as Lord Lieutenant of Essex. The Earl of Oxford went over to the Dutch Prince William of Orange: when he became King William III, reigning jointly with James II's daughter, Mary, he reinstated Oxford and restored all his previous positions, also making him Lieutenant General of Horse and Foot. He was Lord Chancellor (Speaker of the House of Lords) in 1700/01 and died, aged 73, at his Downing Street, London, house in 1703. Oxford was buried in Westminster Abbey in the same vault as his kinsman, Sir Francis Vere.

Pepys knew Aubrey very well when he lived in the Piazza at Covent Garden in 'an ordinary furnished house'. The diarist tells an amusing story about Oxford that he heard at a dinner-table in 1663:

> They talk about a ridiculous falling-out two days ago at my Lord of Oxford's house, at an entertainment of his, there being there my Lord of Albemarle, Lynsey, two of the Porters, my Lord Bellasses and others, where there were high words and some blows, and pulling off of periwigs; till my Lord Monk took away some of their swords, and sent for some soldiers to guard the house till the fray was ended.

The Earldom of Oxford, created in 1142, became extinct on his death and passed, through the representation of his family, to his daughter Lady Diana de Vere, to the Dukes of St Albans. Lady Diana had married Charles Beauclerk, an illegitimate son of Charles II and Nell Gwynne and he was created first Duke of St Albans.

The second Manor of Rivers Hall is a large convenient house about a quarter of a mile from the church. In Saxon times it was held by a man called Grim. After the Conquest it went to Eudo Dapifer, whose under-tenant was Antor.

Eudo de Rye (commonly known as Eudo Dapifer) is

credited with building Colchester Castle between 1076 and 1080 on the foundations of a Roman temple. He was granted the town and it is believed that Gundulf of Rochester, the builder of the White Tower in the Tower of London, was the architect. Eudo, local representative of the Conqueror, also erected the fine Benedictine Abbey of St John in Colchester, which later became so important that its Abbot wore a mitre and sat in Parliament, Kings and Queens being entertained beneath its roof. He also founded the leper hospital of St Mary Magdalene in Colchester and built himself an imposing stone house in Colchester's Roman High Street. Eudo was eventually buried at St John's Abbey, although his heart was returned to his beloved Normandy.

After Dapifer, the Manor progressed through numerous proprietors, with names like Robert de Godebold and Philip de Horkesley. Later, John Breton retained possession for nearly a generation. When Maud, his daughter and heiress, married Sir Richard Rivere soon after 1311, the Lordship devolved to the Rivers family - of great celebrity in Essex, with lands at Stanford Rivers and considerable estates elsewhere.

By 1576 the Manor of Rivers Hall was owned by John Ive, whose son, Sir Mark Ive, sold it to the Bayning family. One of the heirs of Lord Viscount Bayning later sold it to Nicholas Freeman.

Park House is another ancient Manor formerly belonging to the Maidstone family.

There was a charitable bequest made in the village of Boxted in 1637 by Richard Gilder, husbandman, who gave land in Birch, known as Lynefield, and two cottages, for the use of the parish poor. There were also a couple of almshouses in the churchyard for two widows.

In 1968 Boxted had three inns: the Queen's Head, the Cross and the Wig and Fidget, the latter possibly the oddest-named pub in the county. The derivation of pub names is a study in itself and one story is that courts were held here in ancient times. Hence the Wig part of the unusual name. Another tales suggests that a former owner was a Whig, who was an eccentric man – a fidgety person – who used to plough his fields by candlelight.

Modern Boxted, with a population of about 1,400, still retains the character of rural Essex, with modest new housing complexes, fruit farms and agriculture.

St Peter, Boxted

LANGHAM

It is only a short walk from Boxted to Langham. The parish, as its name denotes, is long, stretching from Mile End, once a village within the Borough of Colchester and now more like a suburb, to the Stour. It embraces about 3,000 acres; over a century ago the population numbered 725; a decade later 821 and a few years ago the figure had dropped to 600.

The lands were owned in Saxon times by one Phin Dacas; subsequently by the same Walter Tyrell who, in the New Forest in 1100, slew William Rufus. Then came Henry de Cornhill, then two or three Nevilles. Henry VIII gave the Manor of Langham first to Catherine of Aragon, later to his third and favourite wife, Jane Seymour, who sadly died young after childbirth. Later again, Henry bestowed it upon Charles Brandon, Duke of Suffolk. Charles I sold it to get some of the money Parliament refused him.

Langham has many Constable associations, mostly happy. Langham Church and the old rectory beside it were the secret trysting places of John Constable and Maria Bicknell, who became his wife. The church stands close to Glebe Farm, the subject of several of his well-known paintings and sketches, including the famous picture in the National Gallery which was loaned, in

1937, to the Constable Exhibition at the Tate Gallery. From the summit of the church tower that artist drew his great picture 'Dedham Vale'; his friend, Archdeacon Fisher, was sometime rector of this parish. Constable told another friend and fellow artist, C R Leslie, R.A., that the Glebe Farm was one of the pictures upon which he rested his 'little pretensions to futurity'.

The charm of the woodland scenery around Langham Church is a thing apart; something no language can adequately portray. Plantations of conifers; cornfields; cottages embowered in nooks: open glades, where pheasants wander in dappled sunshine.

Near the church is Langham Hall. It is a large house, noted for its interior panelling, and stands on an eminence overlooking the valley. Nearby is Church Farm, a 17th century building with a storeyed porch.

Down by the Stour is a timber-framed Tudor house with remarkable Jacobean additions, called Valley House. The porch has brackets fashioned like spiral ornaments, while inside the staircase is elaborately carved with totempole-like newels. Altogether a most unusual and fascinating place.

There is another residence called Wenlocks, where once lived John Wenlocks, publisher of a curious account of his suffering through his loyalty to Charles I.

John Constable had many pleasant memories of St Mary's Church, Langham. As a lad he would sit in the church tower and paint, having climbed the ladder which is still the only means of access. From the top of the tower is a glorious view of the Stour valley, Manningtree and Mistley.

Langham is memorable in the story of British art; Constable had been to school at Dedham, a mile or so away, and often walked through the cornfields to this church. He was a friend of the Hurlock family, some of whom were curates here at one period or another. The Reverend Brooke Hurlock officiated for Dr Fisher, son of the Bishop of Salisbury. Dr Fisher bought Constable's masterpiece 'The White Horse' and his uncle gave encouragement to the artist - hence the now famous painting 'Salisbury Cathedral'. Dr Fisher once offered Constable employment as a Langham schoolmaster. The Rev James Hurlock, son of the previous curate, started a school here in 1829 for the instruction of poor girls. The building in the churchyard is still there today.

The tower of St Mary's church was begun in the 13th century and completed with a brick parapet and pinnacles by Tudor builders. The nave has Roman bricks, used again by the thrifty Normans, and the chancel a little pointed window of about 1200. There are some 700-year-old stone coffin lids in the church and a massive timber dug-out almsbox four feet long, possibly Tudor. Two richly carved bench-ends, with crowns and solemn angels, are certainly of the Tudor period. In the chancel are various floor stones to the Umfreville family [1596-1681]. Outside the church is a lychgate, touchingly dedicated to a 'Mother' in memory of her valued care and teaching.

In 1819 John Constable, living in London, responded to an urgent summons from East Bergholt. His wife's grandfather, Dr Rhuddle, was very ill; so he arrived on the London/Ipswich Coach on the afternoon of 6th May, when he learned that the strict Rector had died the night before. Constable later wrote home to his wife, Maria:

> I have been this morning a walk up Langham Hills and through a number of beautiful fields and by the side of the river - and in my life I never saw nature more lovely. Was it not singular that I should arrive in the village just as the bell was tolling for the Doctor - and that his death should have happened on my poor Mother's birthday? - and that the last letter she wrote was to congratulate him on his birthday?
> But I will endeavour to forget those unhappy

divisions - trusting they are now in [a] scene where nothing but peace and joy can reign.

Rev Dr Rhuddle was once Chaplain in ordinary to His Majesty King George III. He was formerly of King's College, Cambridge, and Rector of Brantham, Bergholt and Great Wenham, in the county of Suffolk, for many years. He died in his 86th year and by his will, proved on 22nd July, 1819, Dr Rhuddle left the whole of his personal estate to the Rev William Abbot and the Rev Henry Kebbel (by then vicar of Wistow, Leicestershire), on trust, to transfer £4,000 worth of 3% stock to each of his grandchildren - Samuel, Louisa and Catherine Bicknell, and Maria Constable; Catherine's share being dependent on her marrying with her father's consent. £5,000 was to be paid to his son-in-law, Edward Farnham, under a marriage settlement. Small sums and mourning rings were given to relatives and friends; provision was made for the servants and there were bequests for local charities, including the education of children.

In 1899 Langham was described as a village and parish near the navigable River Stour, over which was a bridge; being four miles from Ardleigh and six from Colchester. It came under the North Eastern Division of the Lexden Hundred & Winstree petty sessions. The rural deanery was at Dedham and the archdeaconry at Colchester (when Essex was part of the Diocese of St Albans).

The Victorians recorded that St Mary's Church was erected at the end of the 14th century on the site of a former Norman church. The church had one bell and 600 sittings and the register dated from 1609. There was a local charity of £13 derived from a 1564 bequest of Thomas Love of Little Horkesley, distributed yearly. Another charity in the sum of one pound, left by Mrs L Dykes of East Bergholt was to provide free education for two children of the parish.

At that time William Nocton, JP, resided at Langham Hall and was the Lord of the Manor; the principal landowners were Mr Blythe of Ardleigh, John Hines of

Lexden, and William Page of Great Horkesley. Crops were wheat, barley, oats, beans and peas and the area of the land was 2,963 acres, with 14 covered by water. There were numerous farmers in the parish: Harry Tollard farmed Park Lane Farm, William Blythe tilled the soil at Martin's Farm, while William Borham was farmer and miller at Langham Water Mill. William Borham, junior, had Little Hall Farm and, for light refreshment, Mrs Ellen Cason kept the Greyhound public house.

W Tolgate was a village grocer and farmer and the versatile Henry Lilley was shopkeeper, grocer and bricklayer. A Samuel Osborn had the country trade as wheelwright and Charles Welbon was the village blacksmith.

There was a Board School (mixed) built in 1848 and enlarged by 1872, for 150 children.

From Langham to Harwich - some fifteen miles as the crow flies, but many more by water - the country is dotted with scenes that Constable drew. Lock after lock from Sudbury to Manningtreee was faithfully depicted by his brush.

The Post Office, Langham

OLD FLEMISH HOUSES, DEDHAM.

Flemish Houses, Dedham, c.1912

DEDHAM

The Dedham of today has much character and charm; no obtrusive building has been allowed to spoil Constable's favourite village. Such houses as have been erected here have been built in a style fitted to these mellow surroundings. In the 17th century Dedham was an important seat of the woollen trade; in Victorian times it had a population of 1,745; and in 1887 it was written of as 'a small, quaint and decayed town, consisting chiefly of one main street, but having some good residences'.

When John Constable was seven, his father began his education by sending him to a school 15 miles from East Bergholt. From there he was removed to become one of Mr Blower's young gentlemen at Lavenham, in the shadow of the great church one of the finest left to us by the medieval cloth merchants of East Anglia. There he had the unhappy experience of being unmercifully flogged by a school usher.

Later he was put in the care of the Rev T L Grimwood at Dedham Grammar School. A portrait of the master, by his famous pupil, is in the Minories Art Gallery at Colchester. John Constable became a firm favourite with the Rev Grimwood, but the only thing he excelled at was penmanship. He had already become so

41

fond of painting that, whenever he paused in the French lesson, Grimwood would exclaim, "Go on, I am not asleep. Oh! Now I see you are in your painting room."

The artist indeed was in his room, to some purpose; certainly far more people know of Dedham through Constable than by any other means. Millions of tourists have visited the area because of his pastoral landscapes.

Dr Grimwood's Grammar School, a red brick Georgian building, is still there on the same side of the street as the church, although it is now two private houses.

Once, writing from Well Walk, Hampstead, in November 1832, Constable told Lucas, the engraver of his English Landscapes series of mezzotints, how the day previously he had travelled from Suffolk in a coach with two gentlemen; all three were strangers to each other. As they crossed the Vale of Dedham, Constable remarked that it was beautiful. One of the pair said, "Yes, sir, this is Constable's country"; so the artist, lest he should spoil it, told his companions who he was.

As a day boy at Dedham Grammar School, he would walk to school each day by the shaded lane seen in 'The Cornfield', which led to a path across the fields, crossing the river from Suffolk into Essex. The education at Dedham was of a high standard and gave him some useful Latin tags to endure through his lifetime; for his mentor, the Rev Dr Thomas Lechmere Grimwood, came from a brilliant family. Both he and his brother were wranglers (a first class man in mathematical tripos), but he had returned from Cambridge to take over the headmastership of his father's school in 1778.

John's father, Golding, was determined to make a miller of him. He had to find a successor to carry on the business and Constable's older brother, Golding junior, had a disability, while his younger brother, Abram, was as yet an unknown quantity. So, later, Constable was employed at his father's mill at Flatford, where he performed the duties required of him carefully and well; he was known in the neighbourhood as 'the handsome miller'. His father wished him to have all-round experience at mill work and later employed him in his counting office, but John Constable left school at the age of 16 or 17 with a burning ambition to paint the scenes he knew and loved so well.

Golding Constable was not, in a sense, an ordinary poor miller, although with a wife and six children to care for, he could never have been rich. When quite young he had a fortune left to him by his Uncle Abram of Bures, who had built up a prosperous business for himself as a corn-factor in Mark Lane, London. By his will, Abram Constable left Golding the whole of his stock in cash and Government securities; furniture and pictures from the house in Mark Lane; and property in East Bergholt - the latter including Flatford Mill on the Stour.

Golding did sufficiently well for himself to acquire another, larger corn-mill at Dedham with an undershot water-wheel driving five pairs of stones, as well as a windmill and roundhouse at East Bergholt. For the purpose of his London trade he occupied two yards on the quay at Mistley, adjoining the Slate House of his Uncle Daniel, a merchant of Manningtree. He also owned the sailing ship *Telegraph*, travelling at regular intervals from Mistley to London. So Golding was not just a miller, but a mill owner, who supervised the work of his mills.

Golding, whose work lay in the counting house, was on a very different footing from Henry Crush, miller at Flatford when Uncle Abram died, and who then passed into Golding's service. It would be more correct to described Golding Constable as a 'merchant', as John did when introducing his father to Joseph Farington, R.A.

Golding's success was due, not only to his keen business shrewdness, but also to his ability to select good men to work under him. "My father's men were hand picked - not men of wood," declared his daughter, Mary.

His steward, James Revans, lived and died in his service and, after Golding's death, his huntsman, old Joseph King, told John that he had thrashed in the same barn every October for the previous seventy years.

Golding Constable must have wondered at times how strange a duckling had found its way among his brood. He took it good-humouredly, however, and raised no objection when John went out sketching with John Dunthorne, a plumber and glazier, who lived at East Bergholt in a little cottage by the impressive gates of Golding's Georgian mansion.

Constable was fortunate that an amazing stroke of luck occurred at Dedham - always the scene of great happiness. Sir George Beaumont came there on a visit to his mother and took an interest in Constable's rather clumsy adolescent efforts. So John went to London in 1795, with his father's consent, to ascertain what his chances of success as a painter might be. Sir George had many connections and John took with him a letter of introduction from Mrs Priscilla Wakefield to Joseph Farington.

So, Constable's first steps on the road to fame had been taken from Dedham. It became the inspiration for many of his famous paintings; 'Dedham Lock and Vale' in 1820 and the 'Valley of the Stour and Dedham' painted in 1800-5. Two others were the 'Vale of Dedham' (now in the National Gallery of Scotland) and 'View of the Stour' (hanging in the Huntingdon Art Gallery, Passadena, California). Dedham can truly be called the heart of the Constable Country.

Regarding Dedham's ancient roots, many historians now believe the Domesday Survey was wrong in recording the name as 'Del-ham' - the hamlet in the dale. They think this description of the place name was either an ingenuous misreading, guesswork or, even, a mishearing. The 12th and 13th century charter documents and Papal Bulls give it as Dyham, Diam or equivalents. Dale is Norse, not Saxon, and does not occur in these parts. Dedham derives its name from Saxon immigrants who came up the Stour estuary and displaced the native British occupants. When the long Roman occupation ended Dedham, like the rest of Essex, fell under the rule of the East Saxon Kings. Danish marauders so encroached upon their powers that, by the Treaty of Wedmore (878), Essex, together with East Anglia, was ceded to Guthrum as part of Danelagh and, eventually, like England at large,came under the domination of Cnut (Canute).

He partitioned off his realm into great Earldoms, Essex being assigned to Earl Godwin. So when Harold, son and heir of Godwin, succeeded to the kingship on the death of Edward the Confessor in 1066, Dedham and the adjacent manors were held by Aluric Camp. Whether or not he rallied to the standard of his liege lord and fell at Hastings, we shall never know. The Dedham fief, like that of Bradfield and Mistley, was granted by William the Conqueror in demesne to Roger de Ramis, a Norman. Compared with its neighbours, Dedham had the lead in extent and cultivated land. There was, at that period, 2½ hides of arable, amounting to some 300 acres. The 32 householders imply a population of about 200, but in livestock - sheep, goats and pigs - besides human inhabitants. There was a new mill, with mud banking to provide a reservoir for a continuous supply of water.

The Manors of Dedham passed through many hands, one outstanding Lord being Sir John Fastolf, who was a general who won renown and fortune in the French wars in the reign of Henry IV. He accompanied the King to Normandy in 1415 and was made Lieutenant of Harfleur, the first town taken by the English army. After Henry's death he continued in France as Master of the Household to the Duke of Bedford, the Regent of France, who kept court at Paris. Sir John had several military commands and was appointed, in 1423, as governor of the provinces of Anjou and Maine. He received many honours, like the Order of the Garter, and built a handsome castle at Caister, dying in 1459.

The wool industry began in the 14th century and many Flemish weavers came over in Edward III's reign. Camden, the historian, records the reception in England

45

in 1568 of Protestants from the Low Countries of Holland, who asked Elizabeth I's permission to settle themselves in Colchester and other places, like Dedham. They first brought to England the art of making those stuffs called 'bays and says'.

Morant, also, gives a letter from the bailiff of Colchester dated 1570, respecting the number of 'Dutchmen' in Colchester: 'which persons', it is stated, 'do weave sackcloth, make needles, parchment, weavours' and such like.

The bay trade was an important part of the commerce of Colchester and extended to Dedham. Old cottages, like Southfields, not far from Dedham church, were used in the manufacture of cloth. Today these are often called the Flemish Houses or Weavers' Corner. This latter, with its mellowed roof tiles and tall brick chimneys, dates from the 15th century. Much timber work is exposed and it is built around a courtyard. At the southwest angle is a rare 15th century bay window.

Southfields is believed to have been a wool merchant's house and factory. The building is of two storeys with attic rooms, and has been carefully restored in recent times. Once owned by the Sherman family, leading clothiers, it is designed on the quadrangular plan of a Tudor mansion.

There is an interesting reference to the Dedham weavers in *The Complete British Traveller* of Walpole (1775): "during the winter," he says, "the poor people of Dedham who are employed in the weaving branch consume such vast quantities of sprats that they are called 'weavers' beef' by the people on the coast."

So Dedham prospered until the Industrial Revolution, when machinery in the north of England killed off the hand-weaving industry.

Regarding transport in Constable's time, there is a letter from his brother, Abram, written in 1821, giving a good guide to this matter. It appears that John Constable wanted to visit East Bergholt for a short April holiday. He was coming alone - probably to paint and sketch - Abram was supplying the accommodation.

"I think you had better come by one of the Ipswich coaches," Abram wrote. "Get off at the Tollgate, Dedham. If you say which day, I will meet you there."

Today there is a good Eastern National bus service to Dedham from Colchester and many Essex seaside towns, like Clacton, Walton and Frinton, run coach trips to Dedham to delight the holidaymakers with, perhaps, their first glimpse of the Constable Country.

In the wide street of Dedham there is much charm, with its straight-faced, wisteria garlanded houses and noble Church of the Virgin Mary, which was built in the reign of Henry VII by Thomas Webbe and his son, John, woollen manufacturers. Their merchants' marks, together with royal badges (portcullis red and white rose) are to be seen on the tower. Thomas has a tomb against the north wall: it has a fine canopy, but the brass border of the tomb-slab has been torn away.

The church is large and very fine, built of brick and rubble, with nave, aisles and chancel. It has a lofty western tower of flint, 131 feet high, battlemented with corner pinnacles and it holds eight bells. A bell would be rung, called the 'Gleaners' Bell', during a fortnight at harvest time, pealing morning and evening to announce the period during which gleaning was allowed.

The font cover is made from timbers of the *Royal George*, which sank off Portsmouth in 1782 with the loss of hundreds of lives. It is said that the timbers were rotten through the neglect of the Admiralty.

John Roger, far-famed as a preacher, was parson here for some time. He was part of the old custom of 'The Lectureship of Dedham'. It is said that a 17th century writer once wept on his horse's neck outside the church for nearly twenty minutes, so moved was he by 'Roaring' Roger's homily. He was a Puritan vicar in the days of James I and Charles I for over 30 years and was one of the most famous preachers of his age, described as 'The most awakening divine in England'. His tomb is in the churchyard and in the chancel is his carved memorial bust, in a niche, wearing a skull-cap, ruff and gown.

The church tower features in many Constable paintings - especially 'Dedham Mill', 'Vale of Dedham' and 'View of the Stour'.

The name of the Sherman family is quite well-known in Essex in villages like Bradwell-on-Sea and, indeed, Dedham itself. In St Mary's churchyard is the tomb of Mary, wife of Edmond Sherman, who built the magnificent Sherman Hall, standing opposite the church. The house has a perfect classic red-brick front of 1735, but the rear is older, probably Tudor. Edmond Sherman, a prosperous wool merchant, founded or endowed a local school for 'poor children' and is in the Charter of Elizabeth I as one of the original governors of the Grammar School.

A Samuel Sherman from Dedham sailed on the *Mayflower* in 1620 to start a new life in Boston, New England. He went with the Pilgrim Fathers, the master of the ship being another Essex man, Christopher Jones of Harwich. There is a story that the *Mayflower* picked up passengers at Harwich, sailed to Leigh-on-Sea to collect some more, and then continued on course going westward to Plymouth, before making her epic voyage to Massachusetts. No-one seems to know the precise truth, but there were certainly many Essex men on board that famous ship, including Christopher Martin of Billericay. The Shermans founded a colony in New England called Dedham, after their English roots, and the celebrated General William Sherman, of American Civil War fame, was one of the descendants.

Inns at Dedham are particularly interesting. The High Street Sun Inn, with stables for horses, and timber framed stairway in its open courtyard, could possibly have been a coaching halt. Now it appears like part of a Tudor cavalcade.

The Marlborough Head Hotel, nearly opposite the

church, is said to be a former Wool Exchange Hall – the business establishment of an important clothier named Edmund Gibson, who was described as a 'dyer' in 1686. Inside are some interesting carved beams. It became an inn in 1704. Constable's artist friend, John Dunthorne, painted the inn sign on one occasion.

There was an historic 'Tuesday Market' held in Dedham for centuries; situated just north of the churchyard it stretched from the Sun to the Marlborough Head, at the corner of Mill Lane.

Dedham did not decay, like Lavenham, when the cloth industry moved northwards, but became a favourite place of residence in the 18th century, with stately 'assembly rooms' on the site of Hewitt Hall.

Farther down the street, on the opposite side to the Marlborough Head, stands the Congregational Church erected in 1871/2, replacing a little Georgian building of 1739. Now it is a pleasant Arts & Crafts Centre – very attractive for tourists.

The Sun Inn dates from the 1500s and has a Georgian brick frontage. It has a resident ghost, believed to have been a witch and was the setting for one of the last witchburnings in East Anglia.

Southfields has a large gateway on the north side through which loaded wagons could pass. By Edwardian times it had degenerated into a very poor tenement divided into cottages. However, since World War II, it has been thoroughly restored and the outside timbers and beams are again revealed in all their splendour.

After passing the Gun Inn at Langham, the Stour turns more directly eastwards; then, in the space of about a mile, it reaches the lock and mill at Dedham. The mill Constable never grew tired of painting has gone, but the new mill and lock remain. Writing of his Stour pictures, Constable said: "My lock is liked at the Academy, and indeed its light cannot be put out, because it is the light of nature, the mother of all that is valuable in poetry, painting or anything else where an appeal to the soul is required."

John's sister, Martha (Patty) married a London business man named Nathaniel Whalley. Later he retired from his business in Aldgate and brought his family to live in Dedham. Either then or later they occupied the small house opposite Dedham Mill. It had been offered to Constable by his father if he would consent to leave London and grow grass roots again at Dedham, but John seems to have declined this generous offer, although he often stayed at East Bergholt with Golding during his long summer vacation.

The mill has had many owners, since Golding Constable owned and improved it in 1776. It was in the hands of Clovers, Ltd. (Flour Mills) until 1984. Now it is being renovated and converted into splendid flats, however, small boys can still be seen fishing at Dedham Lock – just as they did in Constable's day.

There are many places of interest to visit in Constable's Dedham district of Esssex.

The Vale of Dedham Shire Horse and Farm Centre is not far away, one mile south of the village at Barrett's Farm, East Lane. It has superb gardens and meadow walks, and a glorious view across the Vale. It is home for the famous Shire show horses that once could be seen on every farm, but which now, alas, are rare. Also to be seen are Falabella miniature horses; Highland cattle and calves; sheep and lambs; goats; peacocks, etc. Other attractions are a children's play area; demonstrations of driving traps; braiding and grooming; rides on Essex waggons; refreshments and a souvenir shop; a harness room; and some vintage horse-drawn vehicles. Free picnic and car park areas are provided.

Also in the vicinity may be found Castle House, home of the artist Sir Alfred Munnings [1878-1959]. His pictures of horses attracted world-wide renown and were acknowledged as having no rival since the days of Stubbs. A Suffolk-born man, he was President of the Royal Academy from 1944 to 1949. Blind in one eye, he passionately hated what is called 'modern art'. He once agreed with Sir Winston Churchill "that if he saw Picasso coming down a street, he would kick him in the rear end." Sir Alfred painted gypsies and horse dealers, besides society portraits of Masters of Foxhounds. Castle House, with its collection of Munnings' paintings is open on various Sundays in the summer months.

From Dedham there are many short walks by Stourside, including one to Flatford. From the Essex side of the river can be seen three beautiful buildings on the Suffolk banks. First the white farmhouse known as Willy Lott's Cottage; then Flatford Mill itself - a large redbrick house with dormer windows and part weatherboarded mill buildings; thirdly, a thatched cottage next to the little wooden bridge that figures in Constable's 'View on the Stour'.

Willy Lott's Cottage is named after he who lived here all his long life, being buried in East Bergholt churchyard in 1849. It was officially called Gibeon's Farm and Constable commemorated it in many fine paintings - 'The Haywain', 'The Valley Farm' and 'Willy Lott's House',

Flatford Mill dates from 1733, the original mill passing to Golding Constable in 1765; but there has been a mill on this site dating back to the Domesday Book. John's brother, Abram, managed the mill during his lifetime and wrote many letters headed 'Flatford Mill' to Constable in London, giving him all the family news.

The Mill and Willy Lott's Cottage were restored and given to the nation in 1927 by T A Parkington of Ipswich. Both today are leased by the National Trust to the Field Studies Council for use as a centre concerned with courses on painting, local ecology and history.

The 16th century thatched Bridge Cottage, owned by the National Trust, has recently undergone a complete renovation with a £150,000 rebuilding scheme and expects to attract more than a quarter of a million visitors a year. It now houses an exhibition entitled 'Constable at Flatford' to help visitors identify views that inspired Constable. There is a small shop and tea-room and here rowing boats can be hired.

Constable said, "Shakespeare could make everything poetical. He tells us of poor Tom's haunts among 'sheepcotes and mills'. As long as I do paint, I shall never cease to paint such places."

Another interesting saying of his was, "The landscape painter must walk in the fields with a humble mind; no arrogant man was ever permitted to see nature in all her beauty."

Royal Square, Dedham.

Marlborough Head Hotel, Dedham

Dedham Village and Church.

St Mary the Virgin and High Street, Dedham

LAWFORD

Lawford is a village that has lost its ancient centre. The north-eastern part, with marvellous views over the wide sea-like Stour estuary, has merged with Manningtree.

The Manors formerly belonged to Harold II, the last Saxon king, killed at the Battle of Hastings.

The Constable connection is Lawford Place, which Constable visited in 1804, when he was commissioned to paint portraits of the Bridge family. In his mother, Ann's, correspondence to him in London, dated January, 1811, she wrote, "A grand dance at Mrs Bridges', Lawford, on Monday last - upwards of a hundred invitations - everybody in short but this family."

The village church of St Mary is chiefly of 14th century origin. It was enlarged in 1826 and much restored in 1853; in 1887/9 it was subjected to a drastic and destructive transformation by the over-enthusiastic Victorians. The tower is of brick and stone; it was rebuilt in the 17th century. In the chancel are some old stained glass windows and the kneeling effigies of Edward Waldegrave and Joan, his wife, from the Tudor period. The Waldegraves were a very old Essex Catholic family of Saxon origin, who dwelt extensively throughout Essex and Suffolk.

There were two main Manors of Lawford; Dale Hall,

now a housing estate, and Lawford Hall, once the residence of this same Edward Waldegrave, who built the house in 1583. This Lord of the Manor was related to Catherine Howard, fifth wife of Henry VIII. His wife, Joan Ackworth, was private secretary to that fated Queen, who was beheaded for high treason and adultery.

A Georgian brick frontage was added to Lawford Hall in 1756 by a descendant of the Waldegraves.

Between Lawford Hall and the local Shirburn Mill there is an historic early British burial mound, where two urns were discovered when it was excavated. Overshadowed by the railway embankment stands Shirburn Mill - thought to be the only overshot watermill left in Essex. On or near this site was one of the two mills mentioned in Domesday, one Saxon, the other Norman. The Mill, as it appears today, is a timber structure dating from about 1829/30. It was equipped with a wooden millwheel, but this was replaced with one of metal about 18 feet in diameter and probably weighing two tons. Until 1937 this mill was working, drawing its water from two mill-ponds. Sadly, a few years later the wheel was dismantled and taken for scrap to make tanks and munitions in World War II. There is a stream called Shir Burn, fed by a group of springs all along this small valley and the water from one, called Almond's Well, was barrelled up and sent by rail to London in 1846, when the local railway was first opened. This spring water was marketed in the capital, believe it or not, as 'eye lotion'.

Shirburn Mill is mentioned in Kelly's *Directory of Essex* for 1902, as Sherbourn Mill. Then Harry Dunnett was the local miller and, naturally, it was listed as being driven by water.

The Lordship of Abbots Manor and estate at Lawford (a small manor) belonged to the abbots of St John's Abbey, Colchester. At the dissolution of this great Benedictine Abbey the last Abbot, John Beche, refused to give up his holy office to Lord Thomas Darcy, sent by Henry VIII. It is said he became the victim of a stratagem. He was invited to a local Colchester feast and, when present, was shown the warrant of his death. Beche was hanged and, it is said, mutilated at Colchester in the gateway of his own Abbey in 1539. He has since been added to the calendar of saints.

The manor of Abbots passed into the family of John de Vere, 16th earl of Oxford. He was another fine soldier and a General in Henry's reign. He distinguished himself at the siege of Boulogne in 1544 and was one of the peers who supported Lady Jane Grey to be crowned Queen of England and signed in her favour. But before 19th July, 1553, he had declared for Queen Mary, whose Great Chamberlain he became, accompanying her on a progress through London on 30th September, before officiating at her coronation in November.

The 16th Earl also escorted Elizabeth from Hatfield to the City of London when she became Queen. His wife, Margery, was Maid of Honour to Elizabeth, who visited Hedingham Castle in 1561 when she was 28. Her Majesty arrived on 14th August and departed on 19th, progressing on to Gosfield Hall, then the stately home of Lord Rich.

Dale Hall, another ancient manor, was given to Lord Thomas Darcy in 1552. This Lord Darcy came from a very ancient Norman family, who settled in Tolleshunt D'Arcy, which was named after them. In 1590 Elizabeth gave the Dale Hall Manor and advowson of the church to Peter Wilcox and William Wynn.

The village now has a growing population of 3,700, much more than its neighbouring Manningtree and Mistley, which are 500 and 1,860 respectively. The village hall, Ogilvie Hall, stands as a lasting memorial to the great Ogilvie family, who lived at Lawford Place – now a Research Laboratory for Bakelite Xylonite, Ltd.

Mistley Towers

MANNINGTREE and MISTLEY

In 1909 Manningtree was described as a small market
town on the south bank of the navigable Stour. The town,
with its railway station, includes the parish of Manningtree and parts of the parishes of Lawford and Mistley.
There are extensive maltings and a considerable trade
is carried out in iron and timber. But there is much more
to Manningtree than this brief description, for John
Constable had relatives there and here he painted an
altarpiece for St Michael's Church.

Edward Alston of Diss was a relative of Constable's,
being the son of Fanny, daughter of the artist's great-
uncle Daniel, who was a merchant and brewer of
Manningtree. Edward had inherited his grandfather's
Manningtree interests and made a generous offer to the
parish for the painting of an altar-piece to the value of
£200, laying the idea before the Archdeacon and
Churchwardens for acceptance or refusal. In 1821 John
Constable applied for the commission and got the job:
the religious painting, 'The Ressurection', was duly
completed. Constable's two other altar pieces were for
Nayland and Brantham, both in Suffolk.

The altar-piece at Manningtree has an interesting
history. It stayed in St Michael's, in the High Street, until
the church was demolished in 1965. Cleaned and

reframed it now hangs in the church of All Saints, Feering, where Constable's old friend Walter Wren Driffield was for fifty years resident curate.

Constable's brother, Abram junior, writing to him from Flatford Mill in 1832, recorded

> A Mr Page of Manningtree lost his Brig this day week during that gale of wind about 7 in the evening. She capsized at Purfleet with 750 quarters of corn and all lost, vessel damaged, losses about £2,000.

Manningtree (meaning many trees) carried out shipbuilding up to the 14th century.

At Manningtree the quay can be reached at high tide. Mistley, half a mile downstream, has more quays and a good view of the Stour estuary, looking towards Harwich. Below Mistley the estuary gradually widens, until at Wrabness it is over a mile across.

The River Stour at Manningtree reminds one of old sailing ships and barges that plied to and fro up to Sudbury, as in Constable's day. Now hundreds of swans dance on the silvered waters, like a poetical *Swan Lake,* as the sparkling waters roll away down to the cold North Sea. Great mills still stand by the quayside, and the High Street is full of large Georgian houses with pillared porches that evince the past importance of the town, but now give it character. The chapel suffered at the Restoration and was rebuilt on a new site in the main High Street in 1616. Mistley Church Register states 'Old George Pegrine of Maintree by whose labour of care the chapel there was built under God and King James.' The church was of Jacobean style and was called 'a poor brick building' in 1900. It was rendered unsafe and was dismantled. The wonderfully cleaned and restored Constable painting, representing a corporeal Christ floating up from a place of skulls, was later taken to Feering. The parish of Manningtree has returned to Mistley and the Victorian church there now accommodates the needs of both.

Of course, the town is known throughout the kingdom – and perhaps the world - as being the home of the notorious Matthew Hopkins, the Witchfinder General, who hanged sixty poor women in Essex in one year. He died in 1647.

Also at Manningtree was born Ian Maclaren of 'Beside the Bonnie Briar Bush' fame.

Defoe, when at Harwich, sent his horses to Manningtree and so across the Stour over the 'timber bridge'. People in Harwich, he noted, hardly understood him when he spoke of the Stour or Orwell, as they called these rivers 'Manningtree-Water' and 'Ipswich-water'.

Constable's father, Golding, had two yards at Manningtree and Mistley, on the quay, to assemble goods, like flour, for his London trade. From these storage yards the *Telegraph* often sailed. Constable came on sketching trips to Manningtree and it is thought that he drew 'Fishing Boats at Anchor' here in 1822. The picture is now in the Victoria & Albert Museum.

There was once an advanced cottage industry of spinning woollen yarn and weaving baize cloth in this town, but it declined in the 17th century, as in all parts of Essex. In the 19th century farm labourers received a wage of 10 shillings a week [50p] and, to supplement this income, their wives made shirts at 6d [2½p] each or worked in the fields. Girls and boys left school aged ten and some of the 'gels' entered domestic service locally in Essex or Suffolk, or even travelled to London.

Smuggling went on well into Victoria's reign. In 1725 some 50 gallons of brandy and 50 flasks of French wine were seized on the *William and Sarah*, as she was berthed in a hiding place between Mistley and Wrabness, on her return from Norway.

In 1741 dragoons were called in to help suppress the contraband traffic, but to no purpose. In 1782 some 165 gallons of gin were confiscated at Manningtree and, in the year 1783, tobacco and snuff, evidently from Manningtree, were taken to Boxford, Suffolk. After the

Napoleonic Wars large scale smuggling seems to have ceased, although small-scale operators still smuggled contraband and told stirring tales of their secret achievements.

Another ancient industry was malting. An advertisement in 1759 proclaimed that the town malt could be shipped to London daily. It flourished in the 17th century and, by the 18th, had so expanded that the maltsters formed the leading group of businessmen in the district. Famous local trade names were the Normans, Pages, Bridges (who perhaps lived at Lawford Place) and Edward Alston, who by 1791 was one of the two large-scale brewers in the town.

By 1841 the *Temperance Recorder* lamented that there were 17 maltings and, in 1848, the annual duty made was about £50,000.

Today some maltings remain as older local industries, but mostly in the Mistley area. There are Brooks and Messrs. Edme, Ltd. The Brooks family still own most of the quay built by Richard Rigby at Mistley in 1730. The firm has also been milling corn since 1895. In 1919 the first motor lorry was used and, by 1939, a large granary was built at Mistley.

On 10th June, 1813, Constable started a summer holiday at East Bergholt, probably staying at his brother, Abram's, home, Flatford Mill. Daily he went out drawing familiar scenes at East Bergholt, Dedham and Mistley.

In 1817, after househunting in London, where a suitable residence was found in Keppel Street, Constable and his wife, Maria, journeyed down to Suffolk for a summer break. There he was occupied, as usual, in collecting material for his future paintings. He used a pocket sketch-book of medium size, that shows he was at Dedham on 12th August, Ipswich on 27th and that he also paid a visit to Mistley. This Mistley drawing is in the G Davis Collection at the Victoria & Albert, being part of Captain Constable's sale of 1887.

In October, 1827, John again visited his brother

Abram, at Flatford Mill for a short vacation, bringing his two eldest children, Minna and John Charles, with him. John took them to see the shipyards at Mistley of which he was so fond.

Golding's ship, the *Telegraph*, had many adventures on her voyages around the East Coast from Mistley to the London Docks. In 1811, besides being stuck in the ice at Mistley, she was press-ganged in London Dockland. The growing exigencies of the war with France had now led the press-gangs to interfere with the transport of flour to London!

Golding wrote to John telling him of the tribulations suffered by the *Telegraph*. Zachariah Savell, the mate, was impressed from his vessel, then laying at Pickle Herring Wharf on the Thames. It seems the Master, W Franes, had packed up and run away, deserting ship. The *Telegraph* was left in the care of two old men and a child. Golding solved the problem by sending Captain Chandler from Manningtree on the night coach for London to take charge of the ship. This poor man was impressed too and taken away. After much delay and some trouble, Captain Chandler was released and order restored. He and the two elderly crewmen sailed for Mistley and home. Even the weather improved and was kind to them, so they had a safe journey.

Mistley is about a mile from Manningtree. The name means 'wood where mistletoe grew'. In ancient writing it was named as Sedingho or Shedham. No such name as Manningtree appears in Domesday, it bears the title Sciddinchou.

Both places were under Aluric at the time of William's survey. A Countess Albemarle, married to Eudo, Earl of Campaigne, gave it to Albemarle in Normandy. The Manors were reclaimed by King William and given to the Isle, an Earldom of Holderness.

Mistley village has had three churches in its long history. The original medieval church was at Mistley Heath; only a south porch remains. Endowed by Richard

Darnell in 1520, the church roof collapsed in 1710 and it was replaced by a simple building on a new site at Mistley Thorn (a spur of land by the River Stour).

Mistley Hall was rebuilt by Richard Rigby, a financier who died in 1730. The Rigbys had originated from the Stour estuary and, in 1703, Richard was a London linen draper. He received estates in Mistley as part of the settlement of the affairs of the Earl of Oxford. Rigby sold the drapery business and raised funds to invest and speculate in South Sea stock and, with the profits, he improved Mistley Hall. Horace Walpole described it as 'the charmingest place by Nature and the most trumpery by Art' that he ever saw.

In his 1730 will Richard Rigby founded the 'Rigby Charity'. Even today it is still distributed every year and in the 1790s was valued at £2,189.

His son, the second Richard Rigby [1722-88], was Member of Parliament and Paymaster General to the Forces, 1768/84, in George III's reign. He planned a new development in the last part of the 18th century. He had the grand dream of transforming Mistley into a fashionable spa,. such as Leamington or Bath, with 'pump and assembly rooms'. He wanted 'young blades or beaux and ladies of quality' to take the waters and he engaged the renowned Robert Adam to do the designs. Unfortunately Rigby's shortages and deficiencies as Paymaster General came to light, causing a major scandal, resulting in his losing his employment.

So his grandiose scheme never materialised. Only a square of houses were built and the Swan Fountain, where a white stone figure of a swan floats to this day in a round pond, like a lasting monument to the intriguing Rigbys of Mistley.

There is another memorial that stands on Mistley Thorn, which is now known as Mistley Towers. Robert Adam was commissioned in 1776, with some money provided by the first Richard Rigby's will, to alter and renovate the Church of St Mary, erected in 1735. He added the dashing additions of twin towers at the north and south ends, and portico Tuscan columns, surmounted by cupolas with ionic colonnades. Later the church roof collapsed and the nave was demolished. The twin towers were saved for a personal Rigby Mausoleum, but never used for this purpose.

The third Church of St Mary was built on a nearby site in 1870/1. The tower bears a tall spire of 140 feet and contains a ring of 6 bells, one dated 1747 and five of 1898, when they were dedicated on Lady Day in memory of Queen Victoria's Diamond Jubilee. The Gothic church is a fine building of Kentish ragstone in the decorated manner.

The second Richard Rigby knew all the influential people of his day and played host at Mistley Hall to Robert Walpole the Prime Minister, David Garrick the dramatist and the Prince Regent – later George IV.

Rigby retired to Bath; his dreams of a Mistley Spa remained unfulfilled and he let Mistley Hall to the 4th Viscount Galway. The Hall was demolished in 1844, but a pair of Adam lodges of 1782 stand at the entrance of the driveway.

Mistley owes its importance to the Rigbys who set up a thriving port there, with quays, warehouses and granaries – besides some handsome houses, maltings, courtyards and shipyards.

Today, the Common Market has made all the eastern ports busy and Manningtree and Mistley are no exception. Manningtree now has a sandy beach on the waterfront. The Parish Council paid for lorries to bring hundreds of tons of sand for this transplant to attract youngsters and tourists.

The scene down–river at Mistley Quay is of a thriving place, with six dockside cranes and plenty of ware housing. The port deals with many imports, including coffee, timber, copper, lead and zinc. Since 1976, when Mistley Quay and Forwarding Company took over, the port has expanded considerably.

Mistley has a claim to yachting fame. *Firecrest* was built at Rowhedge on the River Colne by Harris Brothers in 1892, as a fast cruiser for Canon Norman of Mistley. She was over 39 feet long, 8 feet 6 inches beam and drawing 7 feet. Constructed of oak and teak, the *Firecrest* was captained by Philip James and had a Rowhedge crew. After passing to various owners, she was bought by Alain Gerbault, the French tennis star and yachtsman, in 1921. The next year he sailed her alone from Gibraltar to New York in 101 days and was the first single-hander to sail the Atlantic from east to west.

The Mistley Quay Workshops are in some old maltings and encompass a group of young artists, potters, book-binders and cabinet-makers. Well worth a visit.

High Street, Mistley

Mistley

St Mary-at-the-Wall

COLCHESTER

Chelmsford is the county town of Essex, being near the geographical centre of the county and close to the capital of the country, London. Chelmsford Cathedral was a parish church until raised to its present status when Chelmsford became a diocese on its severance from St Albans in January, 1914. But Colchester 51¼ miles from London, facing the east coast, historically deserves the honour.

John Constable had relations in Colchester and often visited them. Mrs W Mason was Constable's first cousin and considerably older than him. Her husband, William Mason, was a solicitor and one of the most respected citizens of the town. He had married John Constable's cousin, Ann Parmenter, the daughter of his aunt Judith. The Masons lived at St Mary's House in Church Street, Colchester, not far from St Mary's-at-the-Wall Church. This was an old Tudor house that Mr Mason had refronted in 1802 and this was where Constable probably stayed on his visits to the town.

The Masons had a daughter, Ann, later Mrs Inglis, whom Constable painted as a girl of 16. In 1830 Mrs Inglis came home to her parents' house at St Mary's as a young widow with six children. Ann Inglis' eldest daughter, Jane, when 17, wished to take up painting and

John Constable offered her one of his pictures as an exercise in art. She took up his kind offer and it was dispatched to Colchester on a London-Ipswich coach.

Constable painted St Mary's church tower, but never managed to accomplish any masterpieces in the area.

The church had been seriously damaged, almost to the point of demolition, in the Siege of 1648, because of its position near the massive town walls. It was rebuilt in 1714, further restored in 1871, and is now an Arts Centre. The lower part of the tower remains a fine weatherbeaten structure of flintstone (15th century) with an abundance of Roman brick, but the whole is rather spoilt by the incongruous red brick belfry which the restorers placed on it. The Civil War will always be remembered in Colchester!

There is a fascinating story connected with St Mary's Church Tower. During the Great Siege the Royalists commandeered the town for a period of 76 days, resisting the combined forces of Fairfax without the walls, and discontent and hunger within. In the tower was a great cannon nicknamed 'Humpty Dumpty', manned by a character of folklore, a gunner called 'One Eyed Dick'. Fairfax, the Parliamentarian leader, knew that to bring about the surrender of Colchester he must destroy that Royalist cannon. His heavy artillery scored a lucky hit and brought everything down, including the church tower and the famous nursery rhyme was born.

It will be recalled that the surrender of Charles I by no means finished all Royalist hopes in England, and in 1648 several risings were planned with the idea of at least improving the King's case when the time came for making terms with Parliament. Among the forces was that raised in Kent by Sir Charles Lucas of Colchester. Their first act was to seize the Parliamentary Commissioners and retain them as honourable hostages. Then, after joining with other groups, in particular a large body from Kent under the command of George Goring, Earl of Norwich, they marched on Colchester.

The town's population was Parliamentary in sympathy, but resistance was practically nil; on 10th June the Royalists entered the town for the purpose of perfecting their organisation before setting out for the Midlands in search of additions to their ranks and cause. Little did they realise that when next their columns passed through the walls of Colchester they would be starved to exhaustion, prisoners all.

If the secret of Fairfax' success in this siege be sought, it will be found in his superior speed. So quickly did he move that hardly were the Royalists inside the walls of Colchester than news was brought of his rapid approach on their heels, along the London Road from the Lexden direction. The Royalist forces were divided in two sections; one left the town and took up a position towards Lexden. It was supported by artillery from the walls and one battery in particular wrought great havoc from the churchyard of St Mary's-at-the-Wall.

So fast did events move that on the day following the Royalist entry into Colchester, Fairfax sent them a summons to surrender. The return of his emisary with a blunt refusal acted like a hair-trigger on the Parliamentary forces, who moved to the attack with such promptitude and zeal that the Royalist troops outside the walls had the greatest difficulty in getting back into the town. A considerable number were killed or captured.

Quick to follow his advantage from such confusion, Fairfax carried out an attack on the retreating army. Before the mighty Headgate could be shut and barricaded, several hundred Parliamentary troops had slipped inside. The invaders were killed to a man and both sides settled down to a long siege. Fairfax later sent arrows and kites over the beseiged town with propaganda messages tied to them.

Fairfax swiftly captured the block-house on Mersea Island at the mouth of the Colne, thus cutting off Colchester's water-borne communications with the sea. Undismayed by the loss of these opening moves, the garrison carried on bravely. A windmill was erected on the castle wall to replace those on the outskirts of town beyond the stout walls - though it was subsequently brought down by a lucky artillery shot. Sallies were made from time to time, various devices being used to harrass the enemy. On one occasion a bull was sheathed with a thin coat of lead covered with flax, saturated with pitch and set on fire (which seems very cruel) and sent in among the beseiging forces followed by a small armed party eager to exploit the confusion.

A month elapsed and then hunger and discontent began to do what General Fairfax seemed incapable of performing. On 20th July the first horseflesh was eaten, the carcass being roasted in public in order to boost the morale of the population, which was not very high. It must be remembered that civilian sympathies were mainly with the Roundhead beseigers.

Relations between town and garrison were not improved by the daily arrival from without of appetizing dishes for the Parliamentary hostages; an ostentatious ceremony of trumpets and waving white flags of which we may sure Fairfax took every advantage.

Still the garrison held out and Fairfax sat before the walls content that, whether the town was captured or not, here he held a most important organised Royalist body. The garrison in their turn drew what solace was possible from the fact that, by detaining Fairfax in this part of Essex, they were materially assisting Royalist risings in other areas of the country.

Soon they were eating cats, dogs and even rats, but still the terrible siege wore on - until that black day, 17th August, when the people rose in great numbers and came before the Mayor's House carrying their children, some starved to death. They demanded and begged that he surrender.

Ten days later Colchester fell; all horses (that were left) and bridles were brought to St Mary's Church, all arms and colours were assembled at St James' of East

Hill. Of the 3,471 members of the garrison who surrendered, over 3,000 were accorded 'fair quarter' with special treatment being reserved for the officers. A fine of £14,000 was levied on the town – harsh treatment as during the previous six years Colchester had contributed over £30,000 to the Parliamentary cause: the alternative to paying, however, was to have the town plundered by Fairfax' soldiers. Actually, only £5,000 had to be found and General Fairfax, who was a just man, gave back £1,000 to relieve the poor of their immediate necessities. Most of the fine was paid by the Flemish weavers.

The material damage to the town was terrible indeed. Hardly a church remains not showing evidence of having been rebuilt in the early 18th century. To the south of the town the defenders had deliberately set fire to whole streets to cover their retreat.

The Old Siege House at the foot of East Hill still retains the scars it received during a brave sally by the beleaguered troops towards Greenstead (then a village outside the walls, now a growing suburb of the Borough). The old timber-framed Tudor Siege House is now a fine inn and restàurant, proudly displaying an engraving of General Fairfax in one of its spacious bars.

Sir Thomas Fairfax left Colchester on 5th September, 1648 and devoted the ensuing fortnight to visiting town and garrisons in the eastern counties, being received everywhere as a hero and conqueror. While Fairfax was being feasted and entertained a very different treatment was given to the common Royalist soldier who had been promised fair quarter. The Londoners, especially, were singled out for severity: for the most part they were sent to Bristol to be transported either to Ireland for service of war or as slaves to America.

Until the Parliamentary army was broken up and removed from Colchester, the other prisoners were confined to the churches of Hythe, Grinstead, Wivenhoe and other neighbouring villages. In their long marches to the castles assigned for their confinment they mostly

71

rested for the night in the parish churches. The 'gentlemen' were committed to the custody of individual officers and troopers until they could gain their liberty by the payment of a ransom.

After the siege the remaining Royalists or moderates were driven from the Corporation. Election day would have fallen at the height of the battle, but was postponed for a month. The extremists and leaders of a mob of 1642 triumphed at the election. Henry Barrington, a leading radical, was actually made Mayor - and was succeeded by two of his followers, Thomas Wade in 1642 and John Furley, who, in 1650, returned to the Mayorality he had held in 1638. Furley's son, John, who, as a young Roundhead soldier, took an unsavoury part in an attack on St John's House (the Lucas mansion) was made a councillor. But the Cromwellians did not enjoy their victory for long, as in 1654 Thomas Reynolds, a clothier and an open opponent of Barrington, was elected Mayor.

There is a local story that Oliver Cromwell, later to be Lord Protector of England, visited Colchester soon after the siege. It had been a sharp thorn in the Protector's side: it is said that he held a thanksgiving service in St James' Church and tied up his horse outside on one of the giant iron rings still to be seen there.

During Charles II's reign Samuel Pepys recorded in his diary the events of the Great Plague, which reached Colchester. The town lost 4,731 lives in 1665/6. At this time Pepys ate a barrel of oysters, which he noted were good, 'though from Colchester where the plague hath been so much'. Later he lamented that the plague was raging mightily especially at Colchester where, he added, 'it was believed it would quite depopulate the place'.

Another diarist, John Evelyn, came to Colchester in 1656 on his way to Dedham. He noted it was 'a faire towne but wretchedly demolished by the late siege'. After alluding to the shooting by the Roundheads of Sir Charles Lucas and Sir George Lisle after the siege, he added that, for the rest, Colchester was a 'ragged and factious towne now swarming with sectaries. Their trading is in cloth of the Dutch and baies and saies with Spain. It is also famous for oysters and eringe root growing here about and candied for sale'.

Candied eringe was for many centuries a sweetmeat delicacy for which Colchester was celebrated. It was a recognised product until about 1860. The candy was prepared from the roots of the sea holly (*Eryngium Maritimum*), a curious and beautiful plant growing in abundance on the sandy seaboard of the eastern counties. The thick underground roots frequently grow in the sand or shingle to a depth of three feet. The process of candying was somewhat elaborate and laborious. The historian, Gerard, gives a recipe for it as long ago as 1597. It was such a favourite that Colchester Corporation was in the habit of presenting packets of it to distinguished visitors. In 1621 they gave four pounds of eringe to the Chancellor of the Bishop of London, paying for it at the rate of four shillings [20 pence] per pound. As late as 1795 Queen Charlotte was presented with a box as she passed through Colchester. Sadly, this candy ceased to be an article of commerce during the mid-Victorian period. Its last known maker was Miss Thorn, an elderly maiden lady.

Colchester stands on the right bank of the Colne, which partly encircles it. Second to none in England for antiquarian and historical interest, Colchester holds the proud record of the oldest recorded town in England. Before the Roman Conquest it was the chief seat of the Iron Age British King Cunobelin (the Cymbeline of Shakespeare), who here established a royal mint and chose it as his capital in preference to Verulam (St Albans), probably on account of its strength of position, situated between the tidal Colne and the North Sea. The ancient city covered 12 to 14 square miles and was named Camulodunum.

It stood on a high crest of ground and was a fair, fortified city constructed entirely of timber, surrounded by huge mounds of earth banks. It occupied the top of a broad ridge sweeping down between the Colne and Roman Rivers, reaching as far as Lexden to the west. There Cunobelin ruled successfully for a number of years until AD 41 and built spectacular palaces, showing a certain standard of civilization, when other tribes were still roaming around in warpaint!

After Cunobelin's death and the invasion of the Roman Emperor Claudius in AD 43, Camulodunum's importance was recognised by the victors. They founded the first British 'colonia', given the name Victricenses, in honour of victory and Claudiana in honour of the Emperor. He decreed that a temple should be erected dedicated to his deity.

Camulodunum became an important centre under the new government, with large public buildings, temples, theatres, baths and many houses of stone, tile and timber. These houses had a range of rooms opening up from a corridor or arranged round an open courtyard, and were warmed by underfloor hot air - central heating, Roman style.

Boudicca rose in rebellion in AD 60/1; she and her daughters had been badly treated by the Romans and the lands of Cunobelin's old tribe, the Trinovantes, had been confiscated by the invaders. Claudius was worshipped like a god in this new Province of Britannia; moreover the colony of Camulodunum was unique because its inhabitants held Roman citizenship and the colony was considered to be an autonomous extension of Rome herself. The dispossessed Trinovantes were naturally very resentful, especially as they were treated as slaves and heavily taxed. So, when Queen Boudicca led her tribe, the Iceni of Norfolk, into battle against the Romans, the Trinovantes were quick to join in their cause.

Together they destroyed the Roman settlements at Colchester, London and St Albans and nearly shook Britain free of the hated yoke of Rome. But the might and discipline of the well-trained Roman army triumphed in the end and brave Boudicca's revolt was crushed. She took poison rather than fall into enemy hands.

Although always a major town in Roman Britain, never again would Colchester figure so prominently in national terms as the Capital of Ancient Britain. The Romans started walling in Colchester after the Boudicca debacle making it safe and secure from future attacks. Recent suggestions have offered Camulodunum as the Camelot of the fabled King Arthur.

John Constable would have seen more of Colchester's massive Roman and Norman walls than are left today. Once there were five main gateways in the great fortifications - the Head, North, Balkerne, East and Saint Botolph's Gates. Now only the first early Roman ruin of Balkerne remains. The town walls are constructed of septaria, intermixed with layers of tiles, and enclose an area of 108 acres. The total length was about two miles - a marvellous feat of building contruction - and the average thickness is from 7 to 8 feet, with a height of over 10 feet at various points in the circuit, although now reduced considerably.

The Balkerne Gateway of AD 200 still stands as a lasting monument to Roman skills. It is near the new Balkerne Hill Bypass and an inn, The Hole in the Wall, now stands upon the site of the northern section. The Gateway's foundations have been opened to view, but nothing remains of the centre arch that spanned the roadway. There still remains, on the southern side, the needle's eye used by pedestrians and the guard-room, where the Roman sentries dozed outside in the intervals off duty and from whence they sprang to turn out when the great ones of the army passed that way. Today the little arched passage is again open to the public, after having been railed off for many decades. There is also a good stretch of Roman and Norman town wall to explore in this area.

After the siege, Fairfax turned his attention to slighting, as it was called, the walls and strong fortifications of the town. The visitor will be surprised to find no trace of other gateways, barbicans or towers – and only comparitively meagre portions of the ancient walls. Fairfax' demolition will account for the absence of these antiquities, still found at Chester and York. Fairfax commanded the Mayor to supply 500 labourers, Colchester to pay the cost, to work with spades, pickaxes and hatchets, not only to remove the earthworks and platforms erected by the Royalists for their artillery, but to dismantle the walls to widen their breaches. The object was to do as much as possible in the way of mischief and destruction to make certain Colchester would never again hold out against Parliament in that or any other age. "Never again," said Fairfax, "shall this Town be forced to stand against its Parliament."

The historian, Morant, came to Colchester in 1738 and was Rector of St Mary's-at-the-Wall. He found chests full of documents in the Town Hall (the old Moot Hall); Borough records going back to the 14th century – some even earlier. Most had remained unexamined, until Morant spent ten years studying them to write his famed *History and Antiquities of Colchester and Essex* in two volumes, the standard work ever since. At the time Morant was writing his history a great controversy was raging over the true site of Camulodunum. Some historians followed Camden, who had identified it with Maldon in the 16th century, while others thought it was sited in such places as Great Chesterford or Saffron Walden. Morant argued forcibly it must be Colchester, reasoning that that were frequent findings of small coins round the town – gold silver and bronze – with on one side CAM for Camulodunum and on the reverse CVN for Cunobelin. Morant was correct, but the final proof was not to emerge until almost two hundred years later.

Philip Morant [1700-70] was a younger son of Stephen Morant of Jersey. He came to England to attend Abingdon Grammar School and went on to Pembroke College, Oxford. After two years as preacher to the

76

English church in Amsterdam his long connection with Essex began. From 1724 until 1732 he was curate to Nicholas Tindal, Vicar of Great Waltham, and during this time he published work that attracted the attention of Edmund Gibson, Bishop of London. Encouraged and advised by the Bishop, Morant began his historical research to such good purpose that, since his day, practically all the county histories of Essex have been based on his work.

Colchester is unique among historic towns in the wide appeal of its many historical monuments. Its Norman Castle stands out as the pearl of the collection. It is at the eastern end of the straight Roman High Street, in a beautiful park. One can best approach it through the Cowdray Memorial Gates.

The castle is often compared with the White Tower of the Tower of London, the design of the two having apparently been identical. It was built in about 1080 by the powerful Eudo Dapifer, steward of King William. Dapifer also founded the great Benedictine Abbey of Saint John the Baptist and became known as the King of Colchester. In all he held twenty manors in Essex.

The construction of the castle is of bright red Roman brick, flintstone and septaria. The walls are over 12 feet thick and they were originally over twice as high as they are now. This is all that remains of the largest Norman keep in England, measuring 155 feet by 113 feet, exclusive of projecting buttresses and chapel apse.

The view from the front displays the impressive round Norman doorway arch in all its splendour. The sycamore tree growing above the archway on the roof of a tower was planted in 1815 by the then Mayor's daughter to commemorate the Battle of Waterloo. There are dark dungeons, Roman vaults and even a Norman latrine.

Colchester Castle stands on the site where once the great Temple of Claudius rose. In the 13th century the Sheriffs of Essex used part as a County Gaol. The de Veres of Hedingham held the Castle from 1496 to 1539.

Possibly because of its obvious strength the castle has only twice been under fire; once in the days of King John and during the Great Siege. After that Sir Charles Lucas, Sir George Lisle and Sir Bernard Gascoigne, the Royalist commanders, traditionally were confined in the long vault to the east of the well house. Gascoigne was reprieved, but Lucas and Lisle were shot in the castle bailey, where an obelisk now commemorates the event.

Some thirty years later the castle was sold for £110 to a miserable fellow named John Wheely, who dug out some of the Roman vaults searching for gold or treasure. He did not find any, so started dismantling the upper storeys of the castle and selling the materials for building. Wheeley was eventually forced to acknowledge the superiority of the stout workmanship of the castle and dismantling became a very unprofitable business. Consequently, he sold what was left of the castle to Sir Isaac Rebow, the local Member of Parliament.

Sir Isaac died in 1726, leaving the castle to his 'undutiful grandson', Charles Chamberlain Rebow, who soon afterwards found a purchaser in Mary Webster. She was a wealthy widow and gave the castle to her daughter and son-in-law, Charles Gray, M.P., who was a zealous antiquary and spent much money on its preservation.

Charles Gray died without offspring in 1782 and the castle reverted to James Round of Birch Hall, whose great-grandson was the Rev James T Round of Holly Trees Mansion, Colchester - father of Rt Hon James Round of Birch Hall. Whilst the castle was still in private ownership a museum was opened in the crypt in 1846.

Constable knew the Rebows of Wivenhoe Park, nearby, and must have viewed the castle on his many painting trips to Colchester, although he was not inspired to capture it on canvas. It is more handsome and complete than Hadleigh Castle, a noble ruin, which was painted by Constable.

The whole castle and grounds were bought for £10,000 in 1920 by Viscount Cowdray, High Steward of

Colchester and Member for the Borough in four Parliaments. The Viscount and Viscountess of Cowdray gave the castle and park, not forgetting the nearby Holly Trees Mansion (once part of the ancient castle's demesne) to the Corporation of Colchester. These munificent gifts were vested for the use and permanent benefit of the townspeople for all time, as a tribute of the Cowdrays great affection for the Borough.

For many years the castle remained roofless, its grassy quadrangles under the sky, but in 1935 the keep was roofed over and enclosed. The structure is rectangular with towers at the four corners and the general picturesqueness of the exterior owes much to the charming little turret at the south-west corner.

Today there is an interesting museum in the castle, which houses antiquities, many of which were found in recent excavations around the town. There is a collection of Roman coins and the famous Roman Colchester Vase, probably made in Colchester in about AD 190 and decorated with gladiators and animals. There is also the famed 2nd century bronze statuette of Mercury, found locally at Gosbeck's Farm, Shrub End, in 1947.

Standing in the gateway of the former St John's Benedictine Abbey in St John's Green - not far from where the new Southway Bypass snakes its way outside the town walls to relieve the centre's congested traffic and looking up into the archway vaulting of this once powerful religious house, the marks made by cannon balls during the Civil War Siege can be seen. The Abbey has gone and this fine 15th century gatehouse is all that is left to tell its exciting story. Perhaps the most pleasing and effective use of flint is 'knapped flint and flushwork' decoration seen here.

The gatehouse is a fine example of such work in Colchester and this ancient structure has suvived the dissolution of the monasteries, the siege, 19th century restoration and two world wars. It is now a public monument in the hands of English Heritage.

The gatehouse was built about 1407 and the records state that the Abbot was presented for having taken a piece of land by the King's highway and for building a stone tower upon it for the defence of the Abbey. Henry VIII's first wife, Catherine of Aragon, rested there in 1516 when on a pilgrimage to Our Lady of Walsingham. These must have been very happy days for the great Benedictine Abbey of St John the Baptist.

Regarding the earlier history of the Abbey, it had its origins in a humble wooden church dedicated to St John and became famous because of various miraculous happenings. Lights were seen inside at night-time and voices heard lifted in praise when the church door was locked and it was well known that no mortal being was within. Moreover, the Abbey Chronicle tells us that on a certain Festival of St John:

> A man who was fettered by the King's command, and was maintained by the townspeople in turns, was present there with many others at the celebration of Mass, when suddenly the bolt of his manacles sprang out beyond four or five of the bystanders and the fetters broke with a noise and the man stood free; and the whole town rejoiced at the miracle.

The fame of the spot at the Norman Conquest was such that Eudo Dapifer decided to erect an Abbbey on the site and, accordingly, the opening years of the 12th century saw here a fine Benedictine establishment, which eventually became of great importance.

Morant's *History of Colchester* gives a good account of the Abbey, which held many manors, including those of Vilege, Bricheing (Brightlingsea), Mondover (Mundon), Picheford (Pitsea), Hallingberi and Monkbury.

Besides two caveats of land and two useful fish ponds, there is mention of Bourne Mill, Colchester, about ¾ of a mile away. Some local history books say the stone lodge was later built from parts of St John's Abbey itself. It dates from 1591 and is a dainty little work with elaborate gables treated in the Dutch manner and is often called Monk's Mill by local people. It became a flour mill in the Victorian era and is now owned by the National Trust, being open certain days each week.

Oyster grounds were mentioned too by Morant and these could have been at Rowhedge, East Doniland. A Fair of four days was their right also at the Nativity of St John. They received fees from the estate of Turftin Wifcard, land of Ralph de Broch. From the church of Turnecroft they received a hide of land. In Effe the tithe of wool, cheeses and underwood. In Eton they got a half tithe of the mills. Tithes were extracted from fourteen places, including the Rodings, Berton and Stanford. The benefactors were noble, rich and numerous, like Queen Maud (Matilda). Robert de Romis gave the church of Ardley (Ardleigh); William de Martel presented the manors of Snape and Aldbury in Suffolk.

Conflicts between Church and State had been going on for many years and, at the Dissolution of the Abbey, Henry VIII gave a 21 year lease of the property to Sir Thomas Darcy; later the boy King, Edward IV, gave it to Sir John Dudley, Earl of Warwick, for services in Scotland and France. After the Dissolution it seems to have become a convenient quarry for building stone.

The Abbey was later sold to John Lucas, town clerk and lawyer of Colchester. The Lucas family erected a splendid mansion on the site of the old Abbey, using some of its stone. During the 1648 siege the Royalists made a small citadel of St John's gatehouse. It afforded the defenders the advantage of shooting from an elevated position, under cover and the shelter of walls and parapets. Fairfax was determined to drive them out with delay and ordered an immediate assault on the post held by the Royalists. His troops prepared scaling ladders about 24 feet high and 6 feet wide, so that six men could mount them abreast. The Royalists knocked the Roundheads off the ladders and threw down upon them great stones and brickbats. They defended the gatehouse with great resolution, till Fairfax' soldiers set up their ladders again and went up with great fury and secured the battlements. From that vantage point they hurled grenados (fireballs) amongst the Royalists. A lighted grenade fell into the powder magazine and a fearful explosion followed. The defenders of the gateway, thus being deprived of the means of continuing their resistance, retired into the safety of the town walls. In their retreat, partly in self-defence and partly in exasperation at their successive losses, the Royalists set fire to the medieval suburbs standing outside the town walls, extending from St Botolph's Priory to the North Gate, on the south and south-west frontage of Colchester.

All night, for about a mile in length, the area continued burning and some saw it from a mile distant. A red dusky cloud seemed to hang over the town and, so furious was the fire, that many stately and goodly buildings were reduced to ashes. How the gatehouse escaped being destroyed is a miracle.

During 1648 the Royalist Lucas family suffered much. Their fine house was completely destroyed by Parliamentary forces. Misfortune dogged the family for Margaret, the youngest daughter of Thomas Lucas of St John's, accompanied Queen Henrietta to Paris as one of her Maids of Honour in 1645. That year she married, as his second wife, William Cavendish, Marquis (later Duke) of Newcastle. Afterwards the Royalists lived in Paris, Antwerp and Rotterdam in financial distress. She came to England to plead for an allowance from her husband's confiscated estates.

After the Restoration the Duchess became a figure of ridicule because she wrote such terrible plays (which she said were only for her pleasure). For a contemporary estimate of her drama we can refer to Pepys, who wrote in 1667:

> To see the silly play of the Duchess of Newcastle, the most silly thing that ever came upon a stage. I was sick to see it; but yet would not but have

seen it, that I might the better understand her.

But on a kinder note he also wrote:

> For all the town talk is nowadays of her extravagencies, with her velvet cap, her hair about her ears, many black patches because of her pimples about her mouth, naked necked, without anything about it. She seemed a very comely woman, and I hope to see more of her on May Day.

St John's Abbey grounds are now the private property of the Officers' Club.

St Giles' Church is near St John's Abbey gateway and, perhaps, was used by servants, besides being the Lucas family's place of worship. It is a small building with a little wooden bell turret, an unusual feature for a town church, though common in Essex villages. Parts of the old Norman building remain on the south side. The church is now redundant and belongs to a Freemasons' Society, so is not open to the general public. St Giles' was much visited for the sake of a large marble slab on the north wall, at the east end, commemorating the two Royalist captains executed at the raising of the Siege, who are buried here. The memorial is deeply inscribed and says

> Under the Marble ly the Bodies of the two Most Valliant Captains, Sir Charles Lucas and Sir George Lisle. Knights who for their eminent loyalty to their Soverain were on the 28th of August 1648, by command of Sir Thomas Fairfax, then general of the Parliament Army, in cold blood barbarously murdered.

The memorial illuminates the manner of men who for 76 days held the enemy at bay. On the evening of the day Fairfax entered Colchester Lucas and Lisle were led from the castle, where they had been confined, to the spot now marked by a monument in the shadow of the north wall. First to face the firing party was Lucas, who boldly declared, "I am ready for you; and now rebels do your worst."

Before his dead body had been removed, Lisle was brought forward. He kissed the body of his friend, made a short prayer and then turned to the firing squad. Believing they stood at too great a distance from him he blandly invited them to approach nearer.

"I'll warrant you, sir, we'll hit you," was the response made by one of them.

"I've been nearer you, friends, when you have missed me," was Lisle's response. He fell courageously.

The two bodies were taken away and interred at St Giles. When the church was restored in 1907 they framed two small brasses removed from the coffins found in the Lucas vault. The smaller brass is less easily deciphered than that stating: 'This cophin incloasis the body of the Right Honble The Lady Anne Lucas, who died on the 22nd day of August in the yeare 1660.'

On 13th June, 1648, Fairfax conveyed a letter to Lord Goring, Earl of Norwich, the chief person among the Royalists in the siege:

> My Lord, I have come hither with Parliament forces to reduce those under your command to the obedience of the Parliament. If your Lordship and those under you will instantly lay down your arms, there might be a prevention of much blood that is likely to be spilt, and the town preserved from plunder and ruin.
>
> The evil must lie with you if you refuse.
>
> Your servant
>
> Thomas Fairfax

So had the Royalists surrendered at that stage, Lucas and Lisle might have had their lives spared.

St Peter's Church, with its huge 17th century tower, is in the North Hill area of Colchester on top of the hill that sweeps down towards North Hill railway station. It has illuminated clock faces dating from 1866 set in the red brick tower. The church retains traces of 15th century work and was listed in Domesday. (In 1911 Colchester had 18 operational churches). In the crypt is a mural tablet to the Marian Martyrs of the district, who were burnt between 1555 and 1558. Queen Mary visited Colchester in July, 1553, when she was presented with a silver cup and £20 in gold. Later in her short reign, in the cause of restoring the Catholic faith to England, twenty men and women were burnt to death in the town and the surrounding district, ten on one fateful day, 2nd August, 1557, in two great fires, one in the castle yard and the other just outside the town walls.

The fine High Street Tudor Red Lion Hotel is one of the most historic inns in the town. It still has the centre archway and inner courtyard, with fascinating timber studs and interesting 16th century carved panels now exposed to view. Elizabeth I visited Colchester for two days in 1579 on one of the Virgin Queen's Royal progresses and, no doubt, Her Majesty passed this inn on her way to the old Moot Hall. It was open even then.

The town was all agog and, although the Magistrates had been friendly to Mary, her sister, they were determined not to be outdone by any town in their expression of loyalty to Elizabeth. So the bailiffs and aldermen welcomed Her Majesty in velvet gowns, with caps and velvet tippets. Secretary Walsingham, a great man and Recorder of Colchester, made a speech and Elizabeth received the gift of a double-gilt silver cup, costing twenty marks, with 40 angels in it [Both worth £33.33 in modern cash]. The smallest contributions, in kind or specie, were always welcome by Good Queen Bess, as she knew, none better, the value of money!

No one knows for sure where Elizabeth stayed on her brief visit; probably with the Lucas family in their mansion in St John's grounds.

Now we come to the little church that stood for centuries out in the middle of the High Street. St Runwald's, not far from the Town Hall, was in the historic Middle Row and a tiny shop stood next door. It was of Saxon origin, with added Norman remains, with a north aisle described as a remarkably fine specimen of the Perpendicular. It was much damaged during the siege, after which it lay desolate until 1760, when it was repaired, refitted and used for divine worship again. It was entirely cleared away in 1878. In 1821 Queen Caroline's funeral procession halted there on its way to Harwich and the coffin rested in the tiny church. Poor unwanted Consort of the Prince Regent, later George IV, she was even locked out of Westminster Abbey at his coronation. Now even her body was returning to her native Brunswick. Nowhere did passion more fiercely burn about Queen Caroline than in Essex: on her funeral procession it was continually escorted by sympathetic crowds, even some Whig gentlefolk.

Since Roman times Colchester has always been associated with the military. The end of the Napoleonic Wars brought a garrison to Colchester and the town has been an important military centre ever since.

In 1856, Prince Albert, consort of Victoria, visited the new wooden army camps. The cheering crowds gave him a loyal welcome and about a thousand flags flew over North Hill, Head and High Streets. One of these wooden huts, of the kind that had been used in the Crimea, remains in Military Road. It was open in 1856 as a garrison chapel and is now called Camp Church.

King George V came to Colchester on two occasions during the Great War. He dined with the Mayor and Corporation while passing through the town to inspect the nearby East Coast defences.

In the last decade Princess Anne, Colonel in Chief of the 1st Battalion, Worcestershire and Foresters Regiment, visited them at Colchester. Other royal visitors have included the Queen Mother, the Duchess of Gloucester and Princess Alexandra.

Scheregate Steps in St John's Street is thought to be a postern gate opening through the south Roman Wall of Colchester. Going up these steps to the town centre, one of the personalities recollected is Little Freddie, a midget seafood seller who for many years stood on his pitch at the top of Scheregate – often with a basket or barrow selling fresh shrimps and lovely cockles. He was only about 4 feet high, but a proper Colchester character. He died in 1984 at the ripe age of 90. Born and bred in Colchester, Freddie started work at 8 years old helping Smiths, the local fishmongers. He was often seen around the town pushing a barrow of bloaters, winkles and whelks. Later in his adult life Little Freddie set up in business in the town. He married in 1960, but sadly his wife died just two years later. In 1972 Freddie enjoyed his Red Letter Day, for Mr W Buckingham, then Mayor of Colchester, gave him a special reception at the Town Hall. Mr Buckingham had promised that if ever he became Colchester's first citizen he would take Little Freddie on a conducted tour of the spacious Town Hall and give him a 'slap-up feast'. Later, Freddie Chapman presented the Town Hall with an oil painting of himself, standing at his favourite spot by the top of Scheregate Steps, complete with gaily painted barrow.

My mother's friend, Mrs Sharpe, a Colchester local, often told me strange tales about Colchester's older characters. Marmalade Emma and Teddy Grimes were a famous tramp couple who haunted the district at the turn of this century. They were featured on several local postcards and Mrs Sharpe said that when she was a child Marmalade Emma collared her, forcing her to enter a local shop to get a pennyworth of marmalade in an old jam jar. Mrs Sharpe was too nervous to say 'no' on being confronted by this thin woman, with pots and pans tied on a rope around her waist and sported a lavish 'harvest festival' sort of hat complete with ostrich feathers.

Mrs Sharpe also told me about the 'Two Hannahs'. Sometimes they were also called 'The Silly Hannahs' on account of their habit of walking along, one behind the other, in Indian file. These strange sisters were born locally in 1837 and often seen along the Lexden Road until well into the Edwardian period. One said she was an Indian princess and the other acted as her maid in waiting. Later they dwelt in Stanwell Street and did straw plaiting, making baskets. By 1900 they were living on charity; eventually one sister died and the other entered the Colchester Workhouse.

The Hythe, the harbour of which has been the property of Colchester Corporation from time immemorial, is now part of the Borough of Colchester, being often called Colchester's Dockland in various Essex guides. The name signifies a haven.

In 1955 the last four sailing barges left the Hythe for work in other areas. They were the *Mirosa,* which only the previous years was racing champion of the Thames; the coasters *Centaur* and *Kitty;* and the veteran *George Smeed,* which had been built in 1882. They had been sold away to end their days as timber lighters at Heybridge and the barge yard was to become part of the coal yards and depots of Wrights and Noy.

The Hythe was once a village and the 15th century church of St Leonard's suffered much during the 1648 siege. The large south porch was rebuilt in 1898 and has a room over it. The tower is wooden capped. This church was damaged by the 1884 earthquake, but was repaired and restored by the end of the century. There is a strange tale of four robbers who broke into the church intent on stealing the sacramental plate. Unfortunately for them they were caught and the outraged parishioners confined them in the chamber over the church porch, where they were left to starve to death. One of the congregation, more merciful than the others, crept into the church and gave the robbers a loaf from his own ovens – an act that so infuriated the clergy that he too was incarcerated in the chamber. Five figures are left on the hammer-beamed roof. Are these the five starved men? Or just wooden carvings, as the archaeologists would have it?

In August, 1752, many people at Rowhedge, near Colchester, must have spied a strange sailing ship limping up the Colne, sadly lost and blown upriver with tattered sails. It came to rest on the mudbanks between Rowhedge and the Hythe, when a strange tale unfolded. Some Customs Officers boarded the distressed vessel thinking it was running contraband and demanded that a huge chest be opened. A gentleman told them there were only ladies' clothes in the chest. Not taking his word, they burst open the box and found the embalmed body of a beautiful lady and a case of jewels. They took the man to the Colchester Constables and the body to St Leonard's.

The gentleman claimed he was Lord Dalmeny, who was born and had spent his life in Italy. He had married his lady in Verona under the name of Kitty (Catherine) Canham. Her last wish had been to be buried at Thorpe-le-Soken and the storm had blown the ship slightly off course. It caused quite a stir and people came from near and far to view the lovely lady. Another shock was in store when the Reverend Alexander Gough, Vicar of Thorpe, came to see the lady and discovered her to be his long lost wife, who had deserted him years before. They had both married her and now mourned together. Her grave is still in Thorpe churchyard.

St Leonard's was made redundant in 1984 and closed after 500 years of service to the community.

Once the Colne silted up, in 1697, and navigation terminated at Wivenhoe, about 3½ miles downriver, until they dredged a deep channel for barges to reach the Hythe. The number of vessels registered at the Hythe Port in 1907 was 226 of 7,771 tons. In that year 96 British and foreign steamships and sailing vessels used the port for their cargoes, as well as 352 barges and coasting ships.

The Romans established their port of Hythe further down the River Colne at Old Heath, once a village and now a built-up suburb of modern Colchester. After their long occupation it declined.

The new Hythe Port is a thriving concern and large

cargo ships from Holland, Germany and France import a variety of goods, such as coal, animal foods and fertiliser. In 1984 alone, one million tons of cargo was handled by the Colne ports of Hythe, Wivenhoe and Rowhedge – increased because of the miners' strike.

The Customs Officers are kept busy as ships arrive at the Colne ports from America, China, Taiwan, Ethiopia and Morocco, carrying a variety of exotic cargoes, like rose petals from Thailand, glassware and colourful carpets from Czechoslovakia.

There are many fine timber–framed houses in the Hythe district. Most have been well–preserved and are an important part of the county's heritage. This was a medieval suburb built outside the town walls. Colchester was growing even in those days and the Dutch and Flemish weavers built and carried out their cottage industry in many of these richly timbered edifices with projecting upper storeys.

Colchester in modern times is still spreading and vast new estates have been erected at Greenstead, St Johns, High Woods and other locations outside the original fortified Roman and Norman town walls.

Of course, the Victorians built their suburbs too, and the Edwardians followed suit, with rows of compact terraced houses in the New Town area. The population in the 1960s was over 130,000: it is still increasing rapidly and is anticipated to be some 160,000 by the 1990s.

Colchester is full of attractive historical buildings and the Rose and Crown Hotel in East Street has a rich heritage. It was formerly a 15th century coaching inn for the old Ipswich Road. Long ago this picturesque building stood at the hub of a lively market on which Henry VII bestowed a Royal Charter. On the surrounding land craftsmen plied their trade. Today this architectural gem is still open for trade, boasting a lounge bar with inglenook fireplace and many bedrooms. It has a fine restaurant serving continental food and traditional old

English roast beef!

The Taylors of Ongar lived in Colchester for a time. Isaac Taylor, a Congregational minister, came to Colchester in 1796 to take over the ministry of the Presbyterian Church of the town. The family lived in Angel Lane, now called West Stockwell Street, in the old Dutch quarter situated between the Town Hall and Castle Park. His daughters were poets and Jane Taylor composed her famous poem 'Twinkle, twinkle, little star' one evening while looking out of her upstairs window over the Colchester rooftops. Most of the houses she would have seen are timber-framed and lath and plastered, and lean quaintly.

The Taylors became acquainted with most of the talented people of the neighbourhood and another sister, Anne, described John Constable of Flatford Mill, with the comment: "So finished a model of what is reckoned manly beauty never met with". She also thought Golding Constable's intention of making John a miller 'simply barbarous'.

In 1833 Constable's friend, R Leslie, sailed for America to take up the post of teacher of drawing at the Military Academy at West Point. Constable presented his friend with a parting gift of a water-colour drawing of a Colchester Windmill. At this period Colchester had many wind-driven corn-mills and several water-mills - like Bourne, Middle, Marriages and Cannock Mills. They were all outside the town walls and Middle Mill by the Colne River, in Castle Park, was often known as Chopping's, because a family of the name owned it for a number of years: it was demolished in the 1950s, but one can still see some of the foundations.

Cannock Mill at Old Heath is a pretty weatherboarded structure, but the millpond has disappeared. Although it is no longer working it is well preserved.

Reference has already been made to Bourne Mill (often known as Monk's) and Marriage's East Mill (of Victorian origin) down at East Bridge, which has now been transformed into a smart hotel and restaurant.

Constable would have seen the old High Street Moot Hall, which was not demolished until 1843. The Moot Hall, c.1200, stood where the Town Hall stands today; it had a beautiful carved window and a rather battered (perhaps with use) carved doorway. When the old Moot Hall was pulled down no-one had a good word to say about the rather ugly early Victorian building that rose in its place. This was superseded by the present fine Renaissance style Town Hall that was begun in 1898, the Duke of Cambridge laying the foundation stone. It was opened on 15th May, 1902 by the Earl of Rosebery. The architect was John Belcher, R.A., and the total cost was £62,000. Queen Victoria was shown the plans and graciously gave permission for the Victoria Clock Tower to be named in her honour, as it was after her death.

Outside the Town Hall, Saint Helena looks down from her lofty station, 160 feet above the pavement. The earliest seal of the bailiffs bears her image. The legend associating Helena with Colchester is of a very ancient origin and can be found in the 14th century Town Oath Book. The parentage and birthplace of Colchester's patron saint are the subject of many conflicting claims, but legend says that she was born in Colchester in the year AD 242, her father being the redoubtable King Coel, who was governor of the district under the Romans and in 238 independently seized the government of those parts now known as Essex and Hertfordshire. Eventually, in 260, Constantinus, the Roman general in Spain, came to beseige the town: after a long siege Constantinus fell in love with the beautiful Helena and they were betrothed.

By way of proof of authenticity of King Coel it may be added that four important relics of themonarch were recognised this century. At Lexden a large hollow known as Coel's Kitchen; the Balkerne Gateway was 'Colkyng's Castle'; while Colchester Castle stood upon the site of his 'Palace'. Concerning the fourth relic, there is the following entry in the town's records, dated 1658:

> If the parishioners of St Peters do well and trulie repair 'King Coel's Pump' in ye Red Row, and keep it in repair, they should be paid 5d by ye Chamberlain out of ye Town Revenues.

Also in 1628 the sum of 1s.6d was paid for 'a sword for King Coel', probably for a statue in the Moot Hall.

Back to Helena, who had married Constantinus and had a son, who in due course became Constantine the Great. Constantinus, meanwhile having been elected co-emperor with Maximian Hercules with authority in Gaul and Britain, found that he should marry Maximian's daughterin-law, Theodora. After her divorce Helena made the pilgrimage to the Holy Land during which she discovered the Holy Sepulchre and the Cross. It is in allusion to that find that her Town Hall statue holds the Blessed Cross of Christ. The True Cross is incorporated in Colchester's Borough Arms, with three crowns.

Colchester is so interlinked with the half-legendary times at the beginning of the Christian era that the acceptance of Helena's right to dominate the town not only is polite to the worthy inhabitants, but seems the natural thing. Truth or legend, no-one will ever discover the whole story, lost in the mists of Roman Britain.

Not far from the Town Hall, in St Helen's Lane, is a little chapel named after Helena, which has endured a varied career. In the 12th century it was presented to St John's Abbey with an endowment of 14 acres of land, but by 1290 the mighty Abbot of the Priory was in trouble with the townsfolk for having failed to maintain it in proper condition. The Abbot apparently attached little importance to the legend of its foundation by the saint herself, because the chapel was eventually restored by John of Colchester, who was moved to his charitable act for fear that the sacred building 'should be applied to profane uses'. Henry VIII gave the property to the Colchester Corporation, who subsequently sold the chapel. In Morant's time it was used by local Quakers as a meeting-house. Since then it has been a furniture depository and a mortuary. The chapel has walls of flint, with a course of Roman brick and there are two 13th century lancets (windows).

Old King Coel is a folk-hero, some historians say, who owes his name to the first syllable of Colchester, which was the Saxon name for the town and means simply the Fortress on the Colne or, perhaps, Colonia-Fortress. But his antiquity and high-living remind one of Cunobelin, who was King of Colchester. The Celtic folk-memory was short in some matters and, no doubt, strange tales of a splendid king of former glory hung about the ruins of the colony and its temple - and were woven into dynastic history.

Next to the Town Hall was the splendid building of the Cups Hotel with a Regency ballroom, minstrel gallery and assembly rooms. This was bulldozed in 1972 to make way for a modern block of offices in the High Street redevelopment: this is known as 'progress'.

In his *Moll Flanders* (1722) Defoe laid the early scenes in Colchester. In the novel Moll's second husband was a 'Colchester draper with stylish tastes' and it was at Colchester that she was left by 'a crew of those people they called gipsies or Egyptians'. The novelist owned property in the district and had a 99 year lease on Severallo or Kingswood Heath, which included Tubbiswick and Brinckley Farms. He acquired this property for his daughter, Hannah, who lived upon the income until her death in 1759.

Further along the High Street, past the Town Hall, stands the Edwardian Hippodrome or Grand Theatre, which seated 1,400, and stars of the music hall regularly appeared there from Fred Karno and George Robey to Arthur Askey. Later it became a cinema and was then converted into a bingo hall for a number of years. Now it has been made redundant and some enterprising people are endeavouring to re-open this red plush theatre as a Variety Music Hall once again.

Down the High Street is Mann's Music Shop, established in Victoria's reign. In 1900 they were advertising Pianos, which they still sell today, and also an early hire-purchase system that people called the 'never-never'. Nearly every Edwardian home had a piano and at weekends the family gathered for a sing-song. Mann's also had a record department for seventy years, the oldest in town, which has recently closed. In 1917 the shop got an agreement to sell Regal Zonophone 78s and in 1929 it got the agency to sell HMV records.

The High Street was granted a medieval Borough Charter by Richard I to hold a street market (cattle and general). In 1189 Richard was on his way to Dover en route for the Crusades: he detoured to Colchester, where he met the Burgesses to collect the first payment of his dues for the privilege of granting that Charter and after that it was paid annually. The market stretched from St Runwald's little church in the Middle Row, reaching down to St Nicholas', the 12th century church near the eastern end of the High Street. The church dedicated to the patron saint of children had the custom of a boy bishop for some centuries. It had a projecting clock, which the townspeople called 'the frying pan'. During 1875/6 St Nicholas' was thoroughly restored at the grand cost of £15,000 and a graceful spire was added by Sir Gilbert Scott, who also designed London's Albert Memorial. Sadly the church was demolished in 1954 and the Essex Co-operative Society built a superstore on the site named St Nicholas House. The rear gardens are full of tombstones and public seats from the old churchyard.

In 1863 the cattle part of the market was moved from the High Street to Middleborough, down North Hill. I remember the iron animal pens for sheep and pigs and a Victorian marble drinking fountain of ornate design. It was closed in 1975 and transferred to new enclosed premises at High Woods. Meanwhile the general High Street retail market was not finally banished from there until 1961; it was resited in Culver Street and many other places, like a poor relation. However, it has recently returned to its ancient position in Colchester's main street, so the wheel has moved full circle - at least on Saturdays, when the street is thronged with happy people searching for a bargain.

Concerning transport in the town, apart from river transportation already considered, in John Constable's day wagons carrying their heavy loads were a common sight. They lumbered through the town driven by a wagoner, who was not allowed to drive his team from the canvas covered wagon, but had to supervise from a separate horse. At the top of North Hill there is a public house of character called The Wagon and Horses, after these cumbersome conveyances.

Some stage wagons operated from Ipswich and called at Colchester to collect goods and journey on, via Chelmsford, to Aldgate, London, on certain days each week. They were operating on loads until the middle of the 19th century, when their trade was taken over by the faster-moving railways.

The stage coaches used to carry passengers, letters and smaller parcels. Until 1846 George Samson's Star Stage Coach left the George Hotel, High Street, for Ipswich sharp at nine every morning.

The railway arrived at Colchester from London (Shoreditch) on 29 March, 1843, and handsome cabs had a rank in the High Street, often carrying passengers between town and North Railway Station.

The electric trams appeared in 1904, serving the Borough until 1929, covering routes to Hythe, East Gate, Lexden, Old Heath Recreation Ground and North Station. Later, petrol buses replaced the trams and, today, Colchester Borough Transport and Eastern National fulfill the same public service.

St Botolph's Priory, which stands about 350 yards south of the Castle, just outside the town walls, now comes under the Department of the Environment. These are the most important ecclesiastical relics in Colchester.

Even in their decay they are impressive and in their hey-day must have been magnificent. The remains of this 11th century church consist of the western front, the north and south walls, and pillars and arches separating the nave from the aisles. The western front presents two doorways, one of which is beautifully moulded in five orders. Above the doorways are a series of interlacing round arches which are almost unique in Britain, since they are of brick. The Priory was founded on the site of an earlier church and was the first house of Augustinian Canons in England. St Botolph's was granted many privileges by Pope Paschal II [1099-1118], but it remained a comparitively small and poor foundation. In the 16th century, on the suppression of the monasteries, St Botolph's Priory Church - or, at least, its nave - was used as a parish church, the rest of the Priory and its possessions being granted to Sir Thomas Audley, the Lord Chancellor. The Priory was used as cannonfodder by both sides during the Siege and the parish afterwards united with that of All Saints. That continued until the present church of St Botolph's was built in white brick 'Norman style' about 1836. This church was the first modern place of worship to be opened in Colchester since the Middle Ages and is still open for prayer.

John Ball (executed in 1381) was the infamous priest who was a leader in Wat Tyler's Peasants' Revolt. He made Colchester his place of refuge, as he had followers in the town. Although not the author of the couplet -
    When Adam delved and Eve span,
    Who was then the gentleman?
which was by Richard Rolle of Hampole, he made it famous by using it as the text for a sermon at the out-break of the Revolt.

It is said that the charge brought against him of High Treason was really for heresy.

On a lighter note, 'Jumbo', the water-tower, has recently celebrated its first hundred years. Built between 1882 and 1884 at a cost exceeding £10,000, its height is 131 feet, 5 inches. The structure has been described by many architectural historians as 'confidently ugly' and it is so breathtakingly out of scale with anything raised in the town since the Castle, that it could not fail to become a local institution.

The name 'Jumbo' was accidently conferred upon it by the Rector of St Mary's Church, the Rev Canon John Irvine, whose Rectory it overshadowed in the Balkerne area. He was angrily put in mind of the large African elephant, celebrated in its days and sold to Barnums, the New York Circus, about the time that the foundations of the water-tower were laid. It has now been listed as a building of historic and architectural interest.

Some of the town's most distinguished names occurred in the 16th century.

Dr William Gilberd was born in Colchester in 1544. After studying medicine at Cambridge and abroad, he became Court Physician to Elizabeth I and James I. He is mostly remembered for his work on electro magnetism, that began the scientific study of electricity in England. Gilberd is known as 'the father of electricity' and there is a monument to him in Holy Trinity Church, where he is buried.

Opposite the church is a Tudor building known as Tymperleys, which was once an outbuilding of Gilberd's property. Recently Mr Bernard Mason, a factory owner, presented Tymperleys and a collection of antique clocks to the town.

Holy Trinity Church is famed for its square, rather rare, Saxon tower - and, in particular, for the small arrowhead doorway in its western face. This redundant church is now an interesting local Rural Crafts Museum, set in modern Trinity Square, not far from the new public library beside the new Lion Walk and Culver Street Shopping Precinct.

Another Colchester worthy was Samuel Harsnett, who became Archbishop of York from 1628 to 1631. He was born in the St Botolph's area in 1561, a baker's son. He became a scholar and fellow of Pembroke Hall, Cambridge, and was later Vice-Chancellor of the University. He succeeded to the sees of Chichester, Norwich and York and bequeathed a valuable collection of books to the Borough. His statue is one of six famous local personages standing in niches along a ledge outside the Victorian Town Hall, along with Gilberd, Eudo Dapifer, and Boudicca.

The Roman passion for oysters was great and we know the conquerors exported the Colne oyster to Rome. The first charter of the ancient fishery was granted by Richard I, confirming the existing rights 'from the North Bridge as far as Westhesse'. Although these rights have several times been challenged, they have never been alienated from the town. The most important oyster bed is in the Pyefleet Channel, separating Mersea Island from the marshes of Langenhoe. Here the young oysters are fattened until they attain the standard size required – set by the beautifully modelled 'silver oyster' of the Corporation – below which it is illegal to sell them. The Colchester Oyster Feast, held annually in October, is a function of national importance. Royalty and famous theatrical and film personalities have been invited to the Feast, which is held in the Castle or the Town Hall. The age of this pleasant ceremony cannot be stated with exactitude, but mention is made of an oyster feast in the Chamberlain's Accounts for 1667, when it was held on St Denis' Day, 7th October, when the St Denis Fair was opened. In 1930 the guests numbered 400 and about 10,000 oysters were consumed. Now there is a sad decline of oysters in northeast Essex and, for the feast, many must be imported from other districts or countries.

The second Charter of Charles I ordered the annual election of a 'Mayor of Colchester' in the place of the two bailiffs and varied, as did later charters, the number of aldermen and common councillors. Until the reorganisation of local government in 1974, the officers and members of the Corporation comprised a Mayor, 8

Aldermen, 24 Councillors, a High Steward, a Recorder and a Town Clerk, with various other officials, such as Surveyor, Medical Officer of Health, etc.

The insignia of the Corporation include the largest silver-gilt mace in England (save for Bristol's), dated 1729; the Mayor's gold Chain of Office, 1765; the silver oyster gauge, 1804; a two-handled loving cup, 1673; and even the Mayor's silver theatre ticket, which probably dates from 1704 - when a theatre was built behind the Moot Hall. The existing common seal of brass is a beautiful example of Edward IV's reign and the Mayor's silver seal (formerly the Bailiff's) is of the same date.

The town muniments are of much antiquity and value and were calendered by Mr Harrod in 1865. In 1902 Mr W G Benham transcribed the highly interesting manuscript known as *The Red Paper Book,* originally compiled in the reign of Richard II, but with a large number of later entries. There are early ordinances concerning the Wool Fair and Wool Market. The cellars below the old Moot Hall were let for wool storage.

Among the regulations affecting the officials were stern orders of 1377/8, enforcing similar rules of an earlier date, whereby the bailiffs and others were strictly prohibited from being vendors of wines or beer.

In addition to the oysters and general fishery and a large wool trade, in 1570 Colchester welcomed Dutch and French refugees who established the 'bay and say' weaving industry that flourished until about 1730. There was also a substantial trade in leather, particularly in boots and shoes. By 1900 the chief industries were more varied and included engineering, milling, brewing, clothing and boilermaking - like Paxmans, down the Hythe.

The annals of Essex are rich in examples of individuals, families and companies who have contributed in their way to our industrial history. Paxman Works celebrated their centenary in 1976 and fresh in the memory is James Paxman [1832-1922], whose name is now borne by

Paxman Diesels, Ltd., a subsidiary of G.E.C. Diesel Company. James Paxman was born at Colchester, leaving school at 15 to learn a trade in his father's smithy, fitting and wheelwright's shop at Elmstead. Within five years he was Works Manager of an engineering and iron founding company in his native town and in 1865 became a partner in Davey, Paxman and Davey Engineers. This firm flourished and moved to a new factory on the site of the present Paxman Works in 1876. By his death Paxman was one of Britain's leading engineers and a distinguished and generous citizen of Colchester. James' ingenuity and attention to detail was inherited by his son, Edward, who died in 1949. There are no members of the family in the business now, but the traditional high standards of engineering are upheld and orders are still treated with the care and attention they received from James Paxman a century ago. Now, with a site almost twice the size of the original eleven acres and a work-force that has expanded from 200 to about 2,200, Paxmans manufacture diesel engines (from 274 to 4,000 horsepower); process plant and equipment for the food and confectionery industries, breweries, oil refineries and the mining industry; and even sewage works. The engines are ordered by the Royal Navy, the Ministry of Defence and by British Rail for their highspeed trains - the prototype of which was powered by two Paxman Valenta engines, each developing 2,250 horsepower at 1,500 revolutions per minute. This took the world speed record for a diesel-hauled train by achieving 230 kilometres per hour (143 m.p.h.). Paxmans supply diesel engines to 42 navies of the world and their long connection with the oil industry has included the provision of diesel engines for *Sea Quest,* the offshore drilling rig in the Forties Field of the North Sea.

Current industries in Colchester include Barretts (confectionery), Woods (metal fan makers), and the huge Telecom complex in West Stockwell Street, with tower blocks. Whitecollar enterprises include giant insurance companies like Sedgwick in Maldon Road and Royal London in Middleborough - on the site of the previous cattle market.

Mann's Music Shop

Scheregate Steps

Launch of the 'Lord Nelson', Wivenhoe 15 Oct. 85

WIVENHOE

Wivenhoe is just outside the Colchester boundary, 3½ miles north-east, with its own railway station, which used to be the junction for the Brightlingsea branch.

The settlement nestles on the banks of the Colne and was a member of the Kent Cinque Port of Sandwich, enjoying a large oyster industry, besides shipbuilding, which is still carried on.

Constable had Wivenhoe connections, for at the Victoria & Albert Museum are two pencil drawings by him of Wyvenhoe Park, dated 29 August, 1817. He was then nearing the zenith of his powers and in that year produced one of his masterpieces, 'Flatford Mill on the River Stour' and exhibited 'Wyvenhoe Park' at the Academy. The Wivenhoe pictures were the result of two visits made the previous year to General Rebow. On 21 August, 1816, he wrote from East Bergholt to Maria Bicknell, his bride-to-be, saying he had just returned from the General's, but was to go again. Accordingly, after a short visit to Putney Heath, he returned to Wivenhoe Park. On 30 August, after referring to the thoughtfulness and kindness of the General and his lady, Constable added: "I am going on very well with my pictures for them."

One of these was of the home of his host and hostess, whose daughter he had earlier painted, in 1812. He wrote, "I believe I am to paint the general and his lady at some future time." No further allusion was made to this matter, until in August, 1819, he wrote to his friend, Fisher, "I am under an engagement to paint the portraits of General and Mrs Rebow, at Wivenhoe Park."

Many engravings were done of Constable's 'Wyvenhoe Park'. The painting shows a lofty, rather wide house, set in a park wherein there are deer, tall trees and water with swans and ducks. Despite its name the Park is midway between Wivenhoe and the Hythe at Colchester; on the north it touches the Harwich Road, while on the west it reaches the Colne. The Park was the home of H J Gurdon-Rebow until late Victorian times, when the present red brick Gothic mansion was built. This is now part of the University of Essex complex and, nearby, rise the large grey skyscraper accommodation buildings. The University has held the Park and estate since 1961.

Early members of the Rebow family, who were merchants and woollen manufacturers of Flemish extraction, included old John, who bought Colchester Castle and received a coat of arms. His son, Isaac, made a fortune out of South Sea stock and was knighted by William III. He was Recorder of Colchester and Member of Parliament. His grandson, Isaac Lemyng Rebow, married the daughter of Captain Martin, who owned an estate at Wivenhoe.

The Martins were another adventurous family, for a Matthew Martin [died 1749] was a burgess for Colchester in the second Parliament of George I and the second of George II. He achieved renown as captain of the *Marlborough* in the service of the East India Company. He defended the ship successfully against three French men of war and brought her safely into port with a cargo worth £200,000. For his bravery he received £1,000 reward and a medal set with 24 large diamonds.

Wivenhoe, Wienhou or, perhaps, Wyneho, is a very

ancient name and no-one knows the whole meaning. The last syllable is Saxon, signifying rising or hilly ground. Aluric and two freemen held Wivenhoe in the reign of Edward the Confessor.

After the Conquest the Manor of Wivenhoe was held by Robert Gernon, who had come over with William the Conqueror and held 44 manors in Essex. The head of his barony was Stansted and, when his son exchanged the family name for that of Mountfitchet, this was added to the place name, making it Stansted Mountfitchet. Robert Gernon founded Stratford Langthorne Abbey in West Ham. The family had a long connection with the Forest of Essex: Richard, grandson of Robert, was a Keeper of the Forest, Keeper of the King's House at Havering and all the other royal lodges in the Forest. This office had been given to him by Henry II, with the custody of the Castle at Hertford. He died in 1217 and his son, also Richard, joined the rebel barons against King John, being taken prisoner in 1217. On regaining royal favour in 1236 he was confirmed in the office of Justice, or Keeper, of the Royal Forests. This Richard died in 1258 without issue.

The Manor passed into the keeping of the de Vere family and, when John 12th Earl of Oxford, and his son were executed in 1461, it was confiscated by Edward IV, who granted it to his brother, Richard, Duke of Gloucester, who became the last Plantagenet King of England [1483-5].

His successor, Henry VII, restored the de Veres to the Wivenhoe Manors and Lordships and one of them built a new road from Wivenhoe Heath into Colchester. John, 13th Earl of Oxford, reinstated in his honours and inheritance by Henry VII, had joined him at the Battle of Bosworth Field, leading the vanguard into action. The 13th Earl was made the Lord High Admiral of England, Ireland and Aquitaine, High Steward of the Duchy of Lancaster south of the Trent, Constable of the Tower of London and Castle Rising, Privy Councillor and Knight of the Garter. Adorned with these great offices of state he lived in a grand manner at Hedingham Castle.

The 17th Earl, Edward, was a great favourite of Elizabeth I and is one of the putative authors of Shakespeare, although this has never been conclusively proven. He had been born at Hedingham in 1550 and succeeded his father at the age of twelve. Edward was put under the guardianship of Sir William Cecil, Elizabeth's Secretary of State, whom she later created Lord Burleigh in 1571, when he became her Lord Treasurer.

At the age of 19 the handsome Earl composed poetry and became Queen Elizabeth's Dancing Master. The Queen called him her Turk and, when the Queen opened Parliament in 1571, Oxford attended Her Majesty as Lord Great Chamberlain, carrying her train from Westminster Abbey to the House of Lords. He was a brilliant and accomplished man in all the arts and would play the virginal for Elizabeth at Richmond. In 1573 Edward was living on his estate at Wivenhoe, engaged in some form of literary activity or other, for in one of his letters he terminates with the remark, "... from my new Country Muses of Wivenhoe".

He travelled on the continent and took a great interest in the theatre, in 1580 taking over Lord Warwick's Company of Actors. He was one of the Commission who tried Mary, Queen of Scots, in 1586. Elizabeth later issued a warrant ordering the payment of £1,000 a year for life to the Earl of Oxford and granted a dispensation not to render an account to the Exchequer as to its expenditure. Even Elizabeth's nephew, James I (Mary, Queen of Scots' son) continued this allowance until the Earl's death. Some historians think this was a pension for being a spy in the Queen's Royal Secret Service.

He fitted out a ship at his own expense against the Armada and did battle in the Channel against Spain's mighty fleet. This 17th Earl eventually got into debt and sold the Wivenhoe estate to Roger Townshend, who was knighted at sea for his bravery against the Armada.

From the Townshends the Manorship of Wivenhoe passed by sale to Nicholas Corsellis in the 17th century. He was a London merchant of Dutch extraction, owning property at Layer Marney also. The Corsellis family hold the tradition that they taught the English the art of printing. The story goes that in the 15th century Archbishop Thomas Bourchier persuaded Henry VI to send an emissary to Haarlem, where a printing press had been set up, in order to learn the craft. This agent, a man named Robert Turnour, persuaded a Dutch compositor, Frederick Corsellis, to carry off a fount of letters and accompany him back to England. He started printing on a press at Oxford before that of Caxton at Westminster.

Another smaller Manor at Wivenhoe, called Swaynes, was owned by Walter Devereaux, Earl of Essex [1541-76]. He undertook to conquer Ulster and, in return, Elizabeth granted him the moiety of the County of Antrim, on condition that he maintained an army equal to the Queen's own forces. To enable him to fulfil this obligation the Queen actually lent him £10,000 at 1% interest, but with the forfeiture of his lands in the event of non-payment. The Essex lands he mortgaged to the Queen were the Manors of Tolleshunt Bourchier, Potting and Rushley, Old Hall, Bourchier Hall in Tollesbury, Swaynes in Wivenhoe, and a host of other manor lands. The adventure in Ireland cost the Earl £25,000 (in addition to the £10,000 borrowed from Elizabeth). In 1575 he was appointed Earl Marshal of Ireland, but died the following year.

St Mary's Church, Wivenhoe, with its substantial flint tower capped with a wooden cupola, was erected in the 15th century. It has undergone several phases of restoration. It suffered much from the earthquake that did considerable damage in this district in 1884. The structure is of the Perpendicular style, comprised of chancel, nave with aisles and the square embattled tower. In 1860 the restoration cost £3,000 and after the

Great Essex Earthquake it required to be restored again. There are some good brasses: one to William, second Viscount Beaufort [1507], with effigy in armour under an elaborate canopy; and another, an excellent piece of Flemish work, to Sir Thomas Westerley [1535], Chaplain to the Countess of Oxford. A brass to Lady Scroope [1537], presented as wearing a coronet and heraldic mantle; the canopy is unfortunately mutilated.

In the vestry is a chest, highly embossed and studded with nails, said to be of Flemish workmanship. The cupola on the tower is also ascribed to Flemish craftsmanship and influence. The present ring of six bells was dedicated on 20th July, 1905; these bells were recast from an earlier ring, of the same number, dating from 1802. The church registers date from 1560.

Those interested in architecture should not miss taking a turn along the lane immediately southward of the church. They will be rewarded by the very fine pargetting decorative plasterwork which covers the entire front of Garrison House on the right. This is thought to be the best example in the county of this particular form of decoration. Garrison House has been lovingly restored.

From the high ground about Wivenhoe Cross the ground gently slopes towards a charming little cobbled quay, which is the most picturesque part of the town, with its assortment of fishing boats and yachts. The smooth flowing Colne gives easy access to the open sea, a facility to which it owes its origin. Ships have been built here from time immemorial. During the siege of Scarborough Castle [1644] it was a Wivenhoe ship bringing succour to the beleaguered garrison with muskets, rapiers and other essentials. Later, Wivenhoe mariners did much to frustrate the intentions of certain continental marauders, who were wont to make raids on the Colne shipping. In February 1654/5 a frigate, then being built by Robert Pardy of Wivenhoe, was reported as top-timbered, the builder needing a further instalment of payment, as per contract. Ketches were also being built in the port. Soon afterwards, Wivenhoe vessels were recommended to keep the coast clear of certain marauding 'small Ostenders', as the Wivenhoe men knew the passage amongst the sands around the East Coast. Wivenhoe, in short, is as delightful and unconventional as any town you will find outside Cornwall or Yorkshire. From the quay it appears as a medley of rooftops on a slight hill, crowned by the embattled tower of the parish church and tall shipyard cranes.

Today the modern docks are expanding with Common Market trade, and still some 'K' registered fishing boats put to sea and sell some of their fresh catch to Wivenhoers on the quay. The shipyards still fashion mighty steel ships, but gone are the millionaire-owned yachts of old, such as the famous racing yacht *The Valfreyia*, skippered by Bayard Brown and owned by an American millionaire, or owners like Sir W S Gilbert, who kept his yacht, *Pleiad*, at Wivenhoe.

Sir John Martin Harvey, the actor, was a Wivenhoe worthy [1867-1944]. Both his father and grandfather were very distinguished designers of racing yachts and schooners. Sir John lived at Quay House as a boy, intending to follow the family calling as a naval architect, until he developed a liking for the stage. Famous for touring Shakespeare in the provinces, he was knighted by George V in 1921. In 1932 he published his autobiography in which he wrote of how his father's yachting friends consumed dozens of oysters at luncheon - taken alfresco and washed down with *Perrier Jouet*. He also spoke of smuggling many years ago: "Wivenhoe enjoyed an almost unrivalled position for the purposes of contraband traffic; the revenue man shot in some desperate affray was a tyrant who richly deserved his fate; the smuggler who perished whilst striving to place his kegs in a safe hiding place was a martyr in the popular cause."

Another aspect of Wivenhoe's maritime history was

111

its salvaging. The North Sea, even up until 1870, was poorly buoyed and lit. Fleets of cumbersome square rigged sailing ships, often half full of water, carried the bulk of the world's trade. Many ships converging on the Thames and the Kent, Suffolk and Essex coasts were wrecked. Dozens were driven ashore by winter gales in a single evening; the Colneside smacks, including Wivenhoe's, put to sea to watch out for ships in dire distress. They were intent on assisting or saving the crews and subsequently salvaging their cargoes. The salvaging boats were between 50 and 65 feet long, averaging 22 tons and were all cutter-rigged with large sails. They were powerful vessels and skilfully sailed by mostly owner-occupied skippers with perhaps up to five hands. All had experience and knowledge of the terrible North Sea and its treacherous conditions. Brightlingsea and Rowhedge, both on the Colne, were the main bases of the salvagers, but Wivenhoe, by the mid-19th century, began to figure more prominently, for a bend and a bottleneck in the river's course meant that derelict shipping could reach Wivenhoe, but not Rowhedge. So Wivenhoe became a port of receipt and of salvage.

In Regency times there arrived at Wivenhoe a remarkable, colourful, creative shipbuilder, Philip Sainty, who sold his shipyard at Brightlingsea at the mouth of the Colne and moved his shipbuilding five miles upriver to Wivenhoe. By 1820 his reputation was such that the Marquis of Anglesey, just home from the French Wars after losing his leg at Waterloo, asked Sainty to build him the famed yacht, *Pearl,* one of the champion racers of her time. This started the tradition of yacht building and introduced the Colneside men to the world and rewards of professional yachting, where they quickly made a name for themselves.

These men turned to fishing and salvaging in the winter season and demanded smacks with the style and speed of racing yachts, which they were used to handling. In the 1830s there were accounts of thirty Colneside smacks engaged in one salvage job, but by 1875 there were only eight Colne smacks pillaging the wrecked German ship, the *Deutschland* (of which more later).

Some of the Wivenhoe built and manned smacks were *Celerity* (1831); *Indefatigable* (1808), 31 tons; *Martha* (1802), 15 tons; and the poetical sounding *Running Rein* (1834) of 9 tons.

In 1829 there was on sale on Wivenhoe Quay of 30 casks of butter from *Vrouw Maria,* lately lost on the Cork Sands (out from Harwich on the North Sea coast). A brig was lost on the Gunfleet Sands in 1831 named *Maria* of Scarborough, carrying coals and glass, bound from Newcastle to Sheerness. The crew were taken into Wivenhoe by the salvagers.

In 1834 the shipyard owned by Philip Sainty went bankrupt and was put up for sale.

On 15th July, 1836, there was an advertisement for the sale at Wivenhoe of ship's stores from *Clingard* (120 tons), wrecked on the Gunfleet Sands on passage to Goole from London. Joseph Brown, master and owner of *Good Intent* of Wivenhoe, was charged in 1836 with possessing two jibs from the Barking smack, *Jane,* wrecked on the Maplin Sands on 12th October and completely stripped the next day - according to her owner, James Morgan. The case was committed to Sessions, but what happened at the later hearing has not been discovered.

The German steamship, the *Deutschland,* got into trouble on the Kentish Knock in 1875. She was a 3,000 ton North German Lloyd liner and had sailed from Bremen with emigrants aboard, bound for New York. Southampton was her first port of call. The courageous little tug *Liverpool* from Harwich, commanded by Captain Carrington, saved 155 lives, although more than 60 were lost. The Wivenhoe salvagers were there later, with about 60 men working on the deck or in the cabins. They were fishing up cargo, stripping saloons, and, if one believes newspapers, breaking open passengers' luggage. It was a field day for salvagers.

Salvaging ceased eighty years ago with the increase in steamships, many built at Wivenhoe and Rowhedge. Also having an effect were improvements in buoyage and pilotage and the greater number of lifeboats - whose work still goes on. Lifeboats were established around the Essex coast towards the end of the 19th century. Since then they have been built and maintained at both Wivenhoe and Rowhedge shipyards, in particular at Cook's of Wivenhoe, the former Ironworks in Rowhedge and, more recently, Ian Brown's lower shipyard.

One should not judge those tough ol' boys too harshly, for they really roughed it and slogged hard to earn a living from that unremitting mistress, the cruel North Sea. They were the very fishermen of England, with no modern equipment, but with manpower and sail they harvested the seas and bravely carried out daring rescues that deserve our respect and praise.

Wivenhoe was also the birthplace of George Bryan 'Beau' Brummell, the Regency dandy and close friend of the Prince Regent. This leader of fashion in English society was a great gamester, was often imprisoned for debt and died in poverty, aged 62, in 1840. In Wright's *History of Essex* there is mention of a William Brummell, who dwelt at Wivenhoe in a handsome white brick mansion. Was this Beau's father?

Constable himself had met the Prince Regent, for in a letter dated 1813 to Maria Bicknell, he wrote of attending a dinner in London to celebrate an exhibition at the British Institution commemorating Sir Joshua Reynolds. He said, "The Prince Regent headed the table of perhaps 200 of the highest characters in the country." Those attending the dinner included the poet Lord Byron, the actress Sarah Siddons, Constable's friend and patron Sir George Beaumont, and the Bishop of Salisbury.

John Turner was one of Wivenhoe's best known figures of recent times. He lived from 1897 to 1985 and was the last of the men who sailed and crewed on the royal racing yacht, *Britannia* under King George V. John

114

Turner, from an old-established local family, had the sea in his blood and started his sailing days as a teenager, when he joined the Wivenhoe fishing smack, *Annie*, at the age of 14. In the Great War he served on oil tankers fuelling submarines. Then, after a spell ashore ship building, he started his yachting career, which lasted until 1938. His most famous berth was the *Britannia* that had originally been built for Edward, Prince of Wales, and had great Colneside connections. James and Jack Carter of Rowhedge had captained this slender vessel for many years. The ship had won over 360 prizes, 231 of them firsts, from 615 starts. She was going on for over 40 years old and was a big yacht of 228 tons, with a length of 120 feet and beam of 23. When George V died in 1936 he expressed a wish that his beloved *Britannia* was to be sunk in the English Channel and this was duly carried out.

John Turner also trained, as a boy, in Cook's Shipyard, West Street, Wivenhoe, and during World War II worked on Mulberry Harbours, which were built in Wivenhoe, to help the D-Day landings in Normandy in 1944.

At the old shipyard shipwrights and carpenters used all their skills in constructing dummy wooden submarines to be placed in conspicuous positions around the east coast and its estuaries. This strategic operation was calculated to fox the Germans when they sent reconnaissance 'planes over to spy on British defences.

In 1985 there was a display in the church illustrating the work of the Jubilee Sailing Trust in connection with the *Lord Nelson*, a sailing ship being built at Cook's shipyard. This was followed in 1986 by a visit from Prince Andrew to see progress on this first sailing ship ever designed to be crewed by physically handicapped people. Work on the *Lord Nelson* had commenced in October, 1984, and, when it was completed in 1987 it was the largest vessel of its kind to be built in Britain for the British flag for 75 years. Its cost will have been £2M, the cash being raised entirely by voluntary contributions from large institutions, businesses and private benefactors. The ship will have a permanent crew of 8 and will have a voyage crew of 40, half of whom will be physically handicapped, including up to eight in wheelchairs. Voyages will range from a weekend to ten days running mainly from her home port of Southampton.

In 1986 James W Cook's shipyard at Wivenhoe went into liquidation with the loss of 90 jobs: there appears to be a recession in shipbuilding in our area at this time.

Today Wivenhoe is expanding all the time, with many people employed at the local University of Essex living in this pretty Colneside town in new housing estates. But there is still a pleasant blend of the old and the new: there is a flavour of antique shops and cosy eating houses (one appropriately named The Smugglers), modest super-markets, banks, estate agents and a good bookshop. There is an adequate Eastern National bus service passing through the town from Colchester to Clacton. Wivenhoe has most of the advantages of modern living, besides the rich tapestry of its colourful past.

Finally, there is a small Constable connection with Alresford, a couple of miles downriver from Wivenhoe, Alresford having its own wide creek. St Peter's Norman church was destroyed by fire in 1971 and today only the shell remains. The new church of St Andrew was dedicated by the Bishop on Colchester in 1976.

The 200 year old Hall is delightfully situated in a wooded park and is the subject of a Constable painting. Nearby, at Alresford Lodge, was the site of a Roman villa, probably associated with the Roman fort that stood on the opposite bank of the Colne.

The Two Hannahs

INDEX

Hythe Quay

St Runwald's

High Street, Colchester, about 1910

Colchester Castle, 1830